Planning, Program Development, and Evaluation

Planning, Program Development, and Evaluation

A Handbook for Health Promotion, Aging, and Health Services

Second Edition

Thomas C. Timmreck, PH.D.

California State University, San Bernardino

JONES AND BARTLETT PUBLISHERS

Sudbury, Massachusetts

BOSTON   TORONTO   LONDON   SINGAPORE

World Headquarters
Jones and Bartlett Publishers
40 Tall Pine Drive
Sudbury, MA 01776
978-443-5000
info@jbpub.com
http://health.jbpub.com

Jones and Bartlett Publishers Canada
2406 Nikanna Road
Mississauga, ON L5C 2W6
CANADA

Jones and Bartlett Publishers International
Barb House, Barb Mews
London W6 7PA
UK

Library of Congress Cataloging-in-Publication Data
Timmreck, Thomas C.
      Planning, program development, and evaluation : a handbook for health promotion, aging, and health services / Thomas C. Timmreck.—2nd ed.
            p. cm.
      Includes bibliographical references and index.
      ISBN 0-7637-0062-2
      1. Health promotion—Planning. 2. Aged—Services for—Planning. 3. Human services—Planning. 4. Preventive health services—Planning.   I. Title.

RA427.8.T56   2002
362.1'068—dc21   2002018869

Acquisitions Editor: Kristin L. Ellis
Production Editor: Julie C. Bolduc
Editorial Assistant: Corinne G. Hudson
Typesetting: International Typesetting and Composition
Manufacturing Buyer: Therese Bräuer
Cover Design: Philip Regan
Printing and Binding: Malloy Lithographing, Inc.
Cover Printing: Malloy Lithographing, Inc.

Printed in the United States of America
06 05 04 03 02   10 9 8 7 6 5 4 3 2 1

*This book is dedicated to Ellen.
A special thanks is afforded her for the time,
diligence, and effort given in editing my many
professional works, including this book.*

Contents

CHAPTER 8   Developing Timelines for Planning and Implementation 147

CHAPTER 9   Implementation of Programs, Services, and Projects: Putting the Plan into Action 169

List of Figures

Preface

Planning has been recognized as an important component of all types of administration since Henri Fayol published his works on planning at the turn of the twentieth century. Planning was brought to the forefront of governmental programs in the 1970s with the development of the Comprehensive Health Planning and the Administration on Aging's Areawide Model planning project. The Areawide Model Project developed noninstitutional health and social services for the elderly. Health planning was in its heyday during the late 1970s and the first half of the 1980s because of the Health Systems Agency's (PL 93-641) activities. When PL 93-641—the National Health Planning and Resource Development Act of 1974—was repealed in 1986, planning as it had been known for a decade ceased to be of concern. Hospitals and other major health and social service agencies turned to a new kind of planning—strategic planning.

Operational planning, program development, and strategic planning came to be known as areas with different focuses. Operational planning is budget driven whereas strategic planning usually is driven by competition and marketing concerns. Program development as a component of planning was pushed from the limelight. In the 1980s program planning and evaluation surfaced as a new effort in the health promotion and health education field.

Organizations that embraced strategic planning soon discovered that one major feature is diversification. *Diversification* is creating and planning new services and enterprises to enhance the parent organization's competitive position.

Planning, program development, and evaluation emerged in the 1980s as a key component of health education and health promotion. Planning and evaluation are skills necessary to successful health promotion, health education, and disease prevention services. Health promotion activities are found in major manufacturing industries, aerospace plants, city and county governments, health maintenance organizations, universities, hospitals, private health clubs, church groups, and other large organizations. Health promotion arose out of community health education efforts and now includes an array of activities ranging from health screening to stress management.

A complete range of health promotion, health education, and human services continues to be developed. Some hospitals are developing both an array of health promotion services and a range of services for the elderly. Visiting Nurses' Associations and large home health agencies are augmenting their services with homemaker services, home repair programs, and durable medical equipment businesses. Life care centers and large nursing homes are developing subacute care services, respiratory care units, respite care, hospice programs, and transportation systems. Public agencies of city and county governments are required to plan and develop programs as new legislation is passed and monies are made available for programs. Some of these programs include health promotion for the elderly, blood pressure screening, and smoking cessation and tobacco use prevention programs, as well as drug abuse prevention for inner-city children, health counseling for pregnant teens, home-delivered meals, and medigap insurance counseling programs.

This book functions both as a handbook for the practicing professional and as a text for students taking undergraduate- and graduate-level courses in health planning, program development and evaluation, health promotion, health education, and health-care administration. The book will guide the planner with a straightforward step-by-step approach that will assure success.

Acknowledgments

Thanks are given and recognition granted to my students under-graduate and graduate, for their contribution to my personal growth and learning. Thanks are also given to them for encouraging me to provide a straightforward approach to health planning and program development, which prompted the writing of this book.

About the Author

Thomas C. Timmreck, Ph.D., has published more than 50 articles on health education and promotion, health services administration, behavioral health, and gerontology. He also has published several books, including the first major dictionary of health services terminology titled *Dictionary of Health Services Management*, and *An Introduction to Epidemiology*.

Dr. Timmreck received a Ph.D. in Health Science from the University of Utah; an M.A. in Community Health from Oregon State University; an M.A. in Counseling Psychology: Human Relations and Behavior from Northern Arizona University; a B.S. in Health Science from Brigham Young University; and a Graduate Certificate in Gerontology from the Rocky Mountain Gerontology Center at the University of Utah.

Dr. Timmreck has been an administrator and planner of a county health and social services agency for the elderly and served as an assistant administrator in a nursing home. He developed a Health Behavior Counseling Center, a Health Behavior Management consulting group, and in a major geriatric hospital he was director of planning, program development, and grants. Dr. Timmreck has been a professor in Health Science and Health Administration and Gerontology at four major universities, including serving as Department Chairman of a Health Services Administration program in a School of Health Professions. Additionally, he served as Department Head of Health Education and Health Promotion at a private college. Dr. Timmreck was also formerly a professor of Public Health and Health Administration and Planning at California State University, San Bernardino.

Introduction

Two areas that have had significant planning, program development, and evaluation activities are health promotion and aging services.

The concepts and approaches presented in this book are useful to organizations planning programs and services for any health, human service, or social service population. The focus is on health or social service organizations, with an emphasis on health promotion/health education and services for the elderly. With major concerns about cost and access to health care, health promotion and disease prevention activities should play a major role in the future of health services.

As older population groups continue to dominate the health-care delivery system and the social services of most industrialized nations, the development of services and programs for older adults will continue to be a dominant focus of federal, state, regional, county, and private agencies. Because health promotion and disease prevention services are a major national concern, it is essential to develop more and better services. The viability of hospitals, convalescent hospitals, nursing homes, and senior citizen centers, and other public health services will depend on the ability of organizations to respond to needs. Only about 5 percent of the elderly are in nursing homes, which means that 95 percent of them are still active citizens in their communities. These active seniors need to have their ongoing quality of life enhanced by developing services across the long-term care continuum from wellness and health promotion activities to services at health-care facilities. Thus, planning and program development should be basic to most institutions and agencies interested in providing health promotion activities across the life span.

The age-old question of quality of life versus quantity of life concerns program planners and influences program development. Medical science and public health measures have contributed greatly to the quantity of life by adding years to the average person's life expectancy.

The program development process can contribute to the quality of life by providing needed health and social services.

The concepts, approaches, and techniques in this book have been used in developing health promotion, health education, aging programs, and programs for health and social services. Hospitals, HMOs, nursing homes, universities, health planning agencies, offices on aging, home health agencies, public health programs, and nonprofit community health and human service agencies have used these concepts to plan and develop programs. The concepts presented here are of universal use and offer a broad application for a whole range of agencies, institutions, and facilities.

The flowchart in the Planning Model on pages xxiv and xxv provides the essential steps and a quick overview of the planning, program development, and evaluation process. The text provides detailed information on the various aspects of the planning process. Used together, the flowchart and the details provide the program planner a quick and easy, step-by-step approach to planning, program development, and evaluation.

Planning is fundamental to all phases of administration of health care and social agencies, both public and private. This handbook walks the busy planner or administrator in the health promotion, health care, or social services field through the planning, program development, and evaluation process. The aim is to provide a simple, easy, and straightforward approach, with enough detail, insight, and direction to be successful.

The Planning Model

The *Planning, Program Development, and Evaluation Model* has ten steps that are integrated a chapter at a time into this handbook. Except for *Step 3* and *Step 6*, which are both in one chapter, an entire chapter is devoted to each step and its detailed explanation. The *Model* is presented in its entirety here at the beginning because it is the book's foundation and provides a summary and an overview of the planning process. The program planner does not need to rely on this model alone, however. At the beginning of each chapter the step from the model that is covered is presented again. Every chapter in this book contains many useful concepts, techniques, approaches, and planning questions. The appendices also provide valuable information and materials.

The 10-Step Planning Model

STEP 1

MISSION STATEMENT: General Idea
or Main Purpose

- This is usually based on a general observation, an obvious seen need or interest, or a
need assessment result.

STEP 2

Complete: Assessment and Evaluation
of Organization, Inventory of Resources,
and Review of Regulations and Policies

Internal Assessment

- Does the organization have the ability and
resources to do the project?
- Does anyone care if the project is done,
i.e., administrators or elderly recipients?

External Assessment

- Will the community accept and support
the project?
- What are the government regulations
affecting the project?
- What are the legal issues?
- Are there any zoning considerations?

Resources

- Money and finances
- Building space
- Personnel
- Equipment and materials
- Transportation
- Expertise
- Motivation and commitment
- Management audit
- Support for:
  - —Organization
  - —Community/consumer
  - —Employees
  - —Board
- Plan for evaluation process

Regulations and Policies

- What are the governmental limitations,
restrictions, barriers, and requirements?
- What are the policy limitations, restrictions,
barriers, and requirements?

STEP 4

Need Assessments

- Identify the catchment area, the target
group, the market—the group or population
to be served.
- Complete a community assessment—assess
and inventory existing community resources,
services, and programs.
- Determine the type of need assessment
method or approach—i.e., survey, focus
groups, PRECEDE model, etc.
- Determine items to assess and items and
issues to be covered by the need assessment.
- Develop a need assessment instrument.
- Develop need assessment methods and
processes.
- Establish a training program for outreach
workers/surveyors.
- Train outreach workers/surveyors to conduct the need assessment.
- Conduct the need assessment/survey.
- Analyze and assess the data and findings
of the need assessment.
- Evaluate the importance of the results and
write up findings.
- Determine results of the findings of the
assessment of the community and its
resources and programs.
- Identify gaps in services and programs,
and identify need areas.

STEP 3

Write Goals and Objectives
- For need assessments and feasibility studies

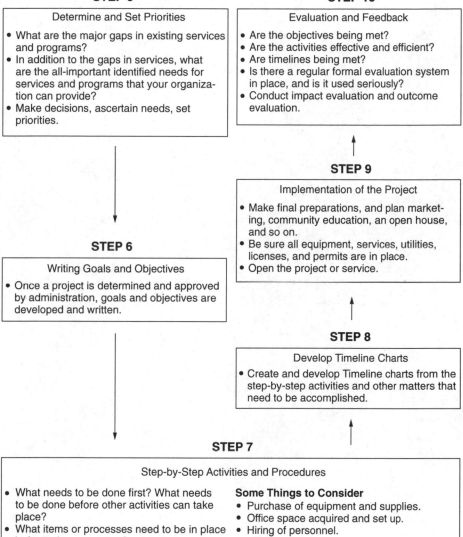

STEP 5

Determine and Set Priorities

- What are the major gaps in existing services and programs?
- In addition to the gaps in services, what are the all-important identified needs for services and programs that your organization can provide?
- Make decisions, ascertain needs, set priorities.

STEP 10

Evaluation and Feedback

- Are the objectives being met?
- Are the activities effective and efficient?
- Are timelines being met?
- Is there a regular formal evaluation system in place, and is it used seriously?
- Conduct impact evaluation and outcome evaluation.

STEP 9

Implementation of the Project

- Make final preparations, and plan marketing, community education, an open house, and so on.
- Be sure all equipment, services, utilities, licenses, and permits are in place.
- Open the project or service.

STEP 6

Writing Goals and Objectives

- Once a project is determined and approved by administration, goals and objectives are developed and written.

STEP 8

Develop Timeline Charts

- Create and develop Timeline charts from the step-by-step activities and other matters that need to be accomplished.

STEP 7

Step-by-Step Activities and Procedures

- What needs to be done first? What needs to be done before other activities can take place?
- What items or processes need to be in place before others can start?

Pilot Projects
- Should a pilot project be developed and implemented prior to committing to a full-blown project? Is a pilot project a logical approach for the project at hand?
- Does the organization have the time and resources for a pilot project?
- Would a pilot project be a waste of time, money, and resources, and therefore it should not be considered? Would a pilot project be a good alternative, and should a pilot project be planned?

Some Things to Consider
- Purchase of equipment and supplies.
- Office space acquired and set up.
- Hiring of personnel.
- Agreements and contracts formally made.
- Legal aspects considered and dealt with.
- Budgets developed.
- Accounting and budget management systems developed.
- Policies and procedures set forth.
- Marketing and community education developed.
- Staffing and organizational structure, meetings, and reporting systems in place.
- Coordination, organization, supervision, and communication systems developed.
- Plans for growth, expansion, and development.
- Forms and paperwork processes developed.

Chapter 1

History and Development of Health Promotion and Social and Health Services Planning and Program Development

ROGER'S RULE

Authorization for a project will be granted only when none of the authorizers can be blamed if the project fails but when all of the authorizers can claim credit if it succeeds.

HARRISON'S POSTULATE

For every action, there is an equal and opposite criticism.

THAL'S LAW

For every vision, there is an equal and opposite revision.

BACHMAN'S INEVITABILITY THEOREM

The greater the cost of putting a plan into operation, the less chance there is of abandoning the plan—even if it subsequently becomes irrelevant.
Corollary: *The higher the level of prestige accorded the people behind the plan, the less chance there is of abandoning it.*

MURPHY'S LAW[1]

CHAPTER OBJECTIVES

The main purposes of this chapter are to present:

1. Health promotion and health education and aging services as models for application to planning, program development, and evaluation.

2. Major developments in planning and program development in health promotion and health education in aging and social services and in health services.

3. An overview of original planning efforts in aging services and the development of program development and evaluation in health promotion.

4. Examples of successful health promotion programs in industry and the community.

5. Examples of successful programs for the elderly.

6. Demographic data and trends in the aging population that are of value to and document the need for health promotion planning and program development.

Health Promotion and Health Education

Early Developments

Health promotion grew out of physical education, school health education, community health education, public health services, and screening and testing in clinical medicine and psychology. The past focus on hygiene gave way to more relevant and educationally sound approaches to assessment and improvement of individual health and the health of the general population. Prevention is the foundation of health promotion—a broad concept with health education as one of the many components. Health education provides awareness, maintenance, and prevention; promotes behavioral change; and spans the gap of knowledge between the consumer and the scientific community.

Awareness is the acquistion of knowledge about health. *Maintenance* is the continuation of acquired positive health habits and the elimination of self-destructive behaviors. *Prevention* depends on awareness and maintenance plus reinforcement of efforts essential to preventing acquisition of new negative risk-taking behaviors. *Behavioral*

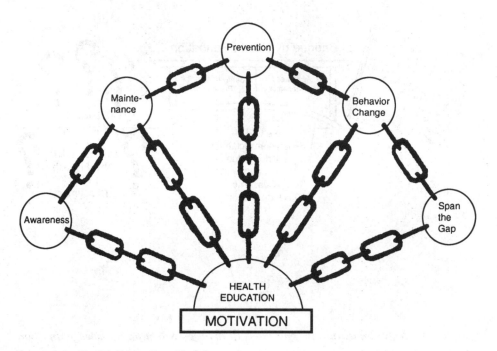

FIGURE 1.1. *Health Education Model*

SOURCE: Timmreck, T. C., Working model of patient-health education, *Radiologic Technology* 51, no. 5 (March/April 1980): 629–635.

change reduces risk factors that are detrimental to overall health status. *Spanning the gap of knowledge* relies on all of the above factors to motivate the consumer to acquire and retain positive health practices and health-enhancing behaviors.[2] Figure 1.1 presents six factors of health education, showing the interlinkage of each with health education and the all-important foundational construct of motivation. Figure 1.2 shows how health education bridges the gap between the consumer and scientific knowledge.

Health education, as defined by the Role Delineation Project, is the process of assisting individuals, acting separately and collectively, to make informed decisions on matters affecting individual, family, and community health.[3]

Health promotion has expanded the concept of prevention, so that it now includes an array of concepts and activities such as health education, health screening, health fairs, employee health status assessments,

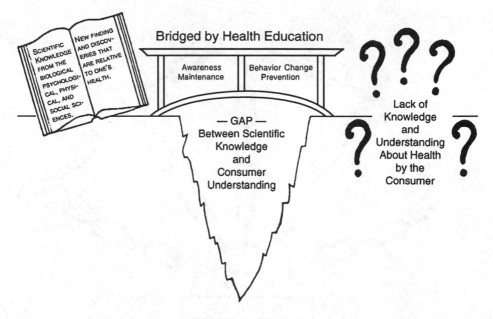

FIGURE 1.2. *Health Education Bridges the Gap Between Scientific Knowledge and Consumer Understanding*

SOURCE: Timmreck, T. C., Working model of patient-health education, Radiologic Technology 51, no. 5 (March/April 1980): 629–635.

smoking cessation help, weight loss programs, fitness activities, safety guidelines, back injury prevention, health counseling, and stress managment. *Health promotion* is defined as the "science and art of helping people change their lifestyle to move toward a state of optimal health." Another definition is "any combination of educational, organizational, economic, and environmental support for behaviors conducive to health."[4] *Optimal health* is defined as "a balance of physical, emotional, social, spiritual, and intellectual health. Lifestyle change can be facilitated through a combination of efforts to enhance awareness, change behavior, and create environments that support good health practices. Of the three, supportive environments will probably have the greatest impact in producing lasting changes."[5]

Figure 1.3 presents key foundational fields used as building blocks of health promotion theory and activities, which in turn provide most of the theory, concepts, and constructs for health promotion and health education.[6] Table 1.1 presents a chronology of developments

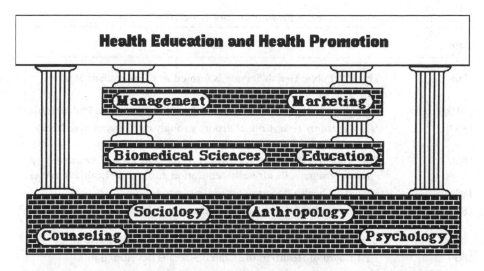

FIGURE 1.3. *Building Blocks of Health Promotion*

SOURCE: Timmreck, T. C., Cole, G. E., James, G., and Butterworth, D. D., The health education and health promotion movement: A theoretical jungle, *Health Education* 18, no. 5 (Oct./Nov. 1987): 24–28.

and lists key individuals who have contributed to the field of health promotion and health education.[6,7]

Services and Programs of Health Promotion

A fairly comprehensive list of services and programs that can be used in health promotion, health education, and disease prevention activities that could be developed in various settings is presented in Table 1.2. Health programs such as these help the worker or individual remain at an optimum level of health. Such programs ensure a higher quality of life; reduce the use of health-care resources; and are useful to help individuals avoid institutionalization, prevent disease and injury, manage disabilities, deal with chronic illness, and prevent untimely deaths.

Many of the programs listed in Table 1.2 have been successfully implemented in hospitals, universities, aerospace industries, large insurance companies, offices of cities of counties, manufacturing plants, high-tech firms, military bases, and other large organizations.

TABLE 1.1. *Development of Health Promotion and Education*

Date	Event
1798	The U.S. Public Health Service is formed as the Merchant Marines Hospital Service.
1815 & 1818	Local health departments are formed in Charleston and Philadelphia.
1837	*Horace Mann First Annual Report* strongly encourages mandatory programs in hygiene in schools.
1850	*The Shattuch Report,* or the *Report of the Sanitary Commission of Massachusetts,* calls for health education and public health activities.
1855	First state health departments are instituted.
1866	Stephen Smith, MD, and attorney Dorman E. Eaton develop guidelines for health departments. They suggest fact-gathering, backing of public health by physicians, popular support, and legislative action.
1869	First Board of Health in the United States is developed in Massachusetts.
1850-1870s	Louis Pasteur and Robert Koch make significant public health and epidemiological discoveries.
1870-1971	Washington, DC, begins a state health department. California begins a state health department. Virginia begins a state health department. Health departments focus on sanitation, control of epidemics, quarantine, fumigation, legal issues, and public policy matters.
1870-1937	Alfred Adler, psychiatrist, develops many leading concepts on mental health.
1874-1949	E. L. Thorndike, psychologist, makes major contributions to learning and learning theory.
1878-1958	John B. Watson, psychologist, founds and develops behavioralism.
1870s-1900	School health education grows rapidly due to Mann's report. Voluntary health agencies grow. Child study movement and public health. Professional associations promote health, education, and professional preparation.
1896-1980	Jean Piaget, child and educational psychologist.
1901	Thomas D. Wood, MD, referred to as the "Father of Health Education," establishes a program of professional preparation in hygiene at Columbia University, New York. First White House conference on health of children convenes.
1901-1978	Margaret Mead, cultural anthropologist and leader in the humanistic psychology movement.
1902	Public Health Service Act organizes Public Health and Marine Hospital Service.

TABLE 1.1. *Continued*

Date	Event
1902–1987	Carl Rogers, psychologist, one of the founders of the humanistic psychology movement.
1902–1994	Erik H. Erikson, renowned child psychologist and developmental psychologist.
1904–1990	B. F. Skinner, behavioral psychologist.
1908–1970	Abraham H. Maslow, leading humanistic psychologist known for his theory of motivation.
1911	Joint Committee of the AMA and NEA on Health Problems in Education convenes.
1912	Public Health and Marine Hospital Service name changes to Public Health Service.
1918	American Child Health Association forms to protect and improve the health of children. National TB Association forms (now the American Lung Association). Sally Lucas Jeans begins health campaigns including public schools. Public health educators at this time were journalists, social workers, nurses, physicians, writers, and so on.
1918	Health education efforts focus on communicable diseases, infant and maternal mortality, poor sanitary conditions. School health education is seen in professional training programs in normal schools. Communicable diseases and poor nutrition kill babies and mothers in high numbers.
1921	*Sommerville* and *Maiden Studies* conducted by Clair Turner clarify the status and role of health education. M.I.T. (Claire Turner) and Harvard University develop health education programs. First M.P.H. degree program starts at M.I.T. Mary Spencer is the first student to complete three degrees in health education, through the Ph.D., Columbia University.
1922	Public Health Education Section of American Public Health Association is founded. Metropolitan Life Insurance Company hires community nurses to help people take care of themselves. Yale University and North Carolina introduce health education curriculums.
1930s	Community organizations (PTA, voluntary agencies) advance the cause of health education in the community.
1931	*Cattagaugus Study*, by Ruth Grout, studies the impact of health education and competency of health teachers.
1935	Social Security Act passes.

TABLE 1.1. *Continued*

Date	Event
1936	*Astoria Study*, by Dorothy Nyswander, on all aspects of school health programs focuses on school health services.
1940	Community organizations demonstrate in North Carolina surrounding World War II efforts, and the needs of workers with communicable diseases. The beginning of patient education focuses on syphillis and gonorrhea. Behavioral science theory and interpersonal process are added to school health curriculum.
1942	Mayhew Derryberry, Chief of Health Education Services (Ph.D. in psychology), assists in the development of the training in behavior theory and behavior change.
1943	School-Community Health Project in Michigan demonstrates effectiveness of comprehensive school-community health programs.
1944	School-Community Health Project in California demonstrates effectiveness of comprehensive school-community health programs.
1945	*Denver Interest Study* gives student need assessment for the development of health curriculum.
1945	Manpower for local health departments is defined by Haven Emerson and Ira Hiscock of Yale University; Yale does research on the matter. Health education training proliferates in schools of public health. 25 schools of public health are now accredited.
1947	460 persons are officially identified as employed as health educators, 300 of them having completed graduate courses in schools of public health.
1948	National Conference on Undergraduate Professional Preparation in Health, P. E., and Recreation convenes to identify competencies needed by health educators.
1949	First U.S. Office of Education Conference on undergraduate Professional Preparation of Students majoring in Health Education is convened, directed by H. F. Kilander.
1950	Official beginning of the Society of Public Health Educators (SOPHE) The National Conference on Graduate Study in Health, P.E., and Recreation establishes guidelines for graduate education.
	Mid-Century White House Conference on Children and Youth recommends greater emphasis on health education in the school curriculum through adequately prepared teachers.
1953	Creation of the U.S. Department of Health, Education and Welfare.
1954	*School Health Education Study* (SHES) in Los Angeles, California, examines the effects of comprehensive school health education.
1956	Two college health conferences are conducted, chaired by Ed B. Johns. The first analyzes health content and methodology; the second studies professional preparation of school heath educators.

TABLE 1.1. *Continued*

Date	Event
1958	*Interagency Conference on School Health Education* recommends effective communication among various elements of health education.
1959	*Highland Park Conference* results in commissions to study specific issues in health instruction, research, intergroup relations, and accreditation.
1961	SHES study surveys about 1 million school children nationwide and initiates the writing of K-12 health education curriculums.
1966	*Committee on graduate Curriculum in Health Education* offers recommendations for a core curriculum to include health science, behavioral science, education, and research.
1969	An interest survey and need assessment, *Teach Us What We Want to Know*, surveys 5,000 Connecticut students.
1970s	Wholistic Health and Wellness Movement Era
1971	Coalition of National Health Organizations forms to mobilize resources of the health education profession.
1972	President's Committee on Health Education forms under President Nixon, with subcommittee on patient education.
1974	Bureau of Health Education, Centers for Disease Control is formed. PL 93-641, National Health Planning and Resource Development Act, is passed.
1976	PL 94-317, National Consumer Health Information and Health Promotion Act, is passed. OHIP Office of the Surgeon General is formed.
1977	National Center for Health Education opens.
1978	National Center for Health Education facilitates the Role Delineation Project. PL 95-561—The Office of Comprehensive School Health Education is created within the Department of Education. National conference on the Commonalities and Differences in the Preparation and Practice of Health Educators convenes in Bethesda, Maryland.
1979	*Healthy People: The Surgeon General's Report on Health Promotion and Disease Prevention* is published.
1980s	Health Promotion Era; health promotion and health education planning and evaluation become a focus of the field.
1980-1985	Initial Role Delineation for Health Education project makes final report in 1985.
1983	Planned Approach to Community Health (PATCH) begins.
1987	AAHE Directory lists 317 professional preparation programs in school and community health education.
1988	National Commission for Health Education Credentialing is formed.

TABLE 1.1. *Continued*

Date	Event
1990s	Health promotion is established with a focus on planning, program development, and evaluation.
1990	First Exam for Certified Health Education Specialist (CHES)
	Healthy People 2000 establishes national health promotion and prevention priorities, and includes health education for first time.
1991	AAHE Directory lists 216 professional preparation programs in school and community health education.
1992	PATCH designates the community health promotion agenda for the 1990s.
1995	National standards for health education Grades K–12 were released. Report on Health Education in the Twenty-first Century was developed.
1999	The title of *health education* was accepted by the U.S. Department of Labor for publication in the *Standards for Occupational Classifications*.
2000	Report of the 2000 Joint Committee on Health Education was published in *American Journal of Health Education*.
2001	Progress report and second meeting of national leaders convened around the Report on Health Education in the Twenty-first Century.

Successful health promotion programs are developed at the worksite or other locations; a few carefully selected programs have been implemented in some companies. On the other hand, a whole array of the programs were needed to make a comprehensive health promotion program for one major organization. Some organizations prefer a multifaceted approach to meet the specific needs of the target population.

A comprehensive health promotion program is the preferred approach for the preventive aspects of the program to be successful and effective. Having just a weight loss program because workers prefer it, or because it is good for morale and employee incentive programs, may not meet the health needs of the target population. The underlying aim of any health promotion program is disease prevention and behavioral changes to improve the health of workers which in turn reduces the use and costs of health services. At the minimum, a health promotion program at a major worksite should include all activities marked with an asterisk (*) in Table 1.2. All health promotion endeavors should start with a need determination process. Appraisals of health risk and health screening should be the beginning steps. This helps establish a baseline of data to demonstrate improvements later, to identify the types of programs needed, and to identify which programs should be implemented first.

TABLE 1.2. *Health Promotion Programs, Services, and Activities*

- Aerobic fitness and exercise, low impact
- Aerobic fitness, dance, and exercise, high impact*
- Aerobic swimming
- Alcohol counseling groups
- Alcoholics Anonymous onsite
- Back injury prevention programs*
- Bicycling programs
- Blood pressure control programs*
- Blood pressure reduction education program for special population (i.e., black males)
- Child health and development classes for parents
- Cholesterol screening and periodic checks
- Communication system—newsletters, videotapes, mailing-system inserts in pay envelopes, bulletin board*
- Drug counseling groups
- Drugs and pharmaceuticals use education, especially for the elderly
- Employee incentive programs (contests for stop smoking, lose weight, use seat belts, exercise, safety accomplishments, and so on)
- Exercise and fitness programs (organized)*
- First aid training
- General health counseling*
- Group therapy for drug rehabilitation
- Health education classes on selected topics*
- Health education programs for high-risk or target groups
- Health fairs
- Health insurance education and counseling for the elderly
- Health risk appraisals*
- Health education programs in Spanish or other language of target population
- Nutrition assessment*
- Nutrition counseling *
- Nutrition education*
- Peer counseling programs
- Risk management programs*
- Running programs
- Safe driving programs
- Safety courses*
- Screening programs—cholesterol, stress, blood pressure, fitness, back fitness, posture analysis, and so on*
- Seat belt use programs

TABLE 1.2. *Continued*

- Smoking cessation, group approach*
- Smoking cessation, individual health counseling approach
- Smoking cessation, targeted groups—i.e., young mothers, minority teens, and others
- Stress management, group approach*
- Stress management, individual health counseling approach
- Support groups of various types, work- or family-related
- Surveys, interest, preference, need assessment*
- Time management and stress management*
- Walking for fitness
- Weight loss, group approach*
- Weight loss, individual health counseling approach

*Suggested for a comprehensive health promotion program.

Aging and Social Service Planning

Historical Events

Historically, there was little concern about persons growing old; life expectancy was short and few people reached old age. If a person was lucky enough to escape the scourges of the life-threatening communicable diseases of the time, then the family would take care of the elderly person until he or she died. Sometimes the very ill and poor were placed in old folks' homes and other institutions—later identified as nursing homes. As communicable diseases were identified, and it became understood how pathogens spread and were controlled, life expectancy increased. The cleaning up of water supplies, garbage, and sewers, plus the inspection and protection of food, eliminated many early deaths. Advancements in sanitation and other public health measures and in the medical sciences made it possible for many persons to live into old age. People began to live long enough to experience one or more chronic diseases, which led to disabilities and required more support in the home, or if serious enough, placement in an institution for long-term care.

In the 1950s and 1960s, order adults and policymakers faced many health-care dilemmas not experienced in the past. People began living into old age in large numbers and a good percentage were ill and frail. They outlived not only their parents but also other family members including their children. Many of these people were to the point of needing care with no one to care for them. For them, nursing homes seemed the only alternative.

Throughout the 1950s and 1960s, long-term care facilities of various kinds and arrangements began to pop up around the country. Some old folks' homes were just large old houses that provided care for 10 to 20 residents. Others were newly constructed convalescent hospitals with nurses and medical and social support personnel on staff.

Many fires and unwarranted deaths in old and unregulated homes, along with widespread stories of abuses in nursing homes, came to the attention of the U.S. Congress. The First White House Conference on Aging in 1961 determined that the U.S. government needed federal laws and funding in order to develop a nationwide system of health and social services for older adults. These support services would create programs to help people remain in their homes as long as possible. Institutionalization costs the elderly their freedom and dignity and is extremely expensive when compared to remaining in one's own home.

In 1965 the Older Americans Act was passed. Money was allocated to develop Areawide Model Projects. These projects conducted need assessments, planning, and program development of the health and social support services for older people. These services had a two-fold purpose. The first aim was to reduce institutionalization, which was not only costly but often unnecessary. The second was to help the aged remain in their homes as long as possible. Gerontologists found that it was best for them to stay in familiar surroundings near family and friends. Thus, a full complement of services was developed to allow the elderly to remain at home and retain dignity and independence.

The Areawide Model Projects evolved into the Area Agency on Aging (AAA's or Triple "A"s). Triple "A"s were established at the grass roots and often were administered by the county or city government. Area Agency on Aging programs were the administrative entities established to manage the newly developed support services.

Because reports to the U.S. Congress indicated that the first and foremost concern was the nutritional status of older people, need assessments as a part of the planning processes under the Areawide Model Projects focused on these needs. The first programs slated for development were home-delivered meals and congregate dining centers. Eventually, a whole continuum of services was put in place in most AAA's (see Figure 1.4). In addition to Triple "A"s, many agencies,

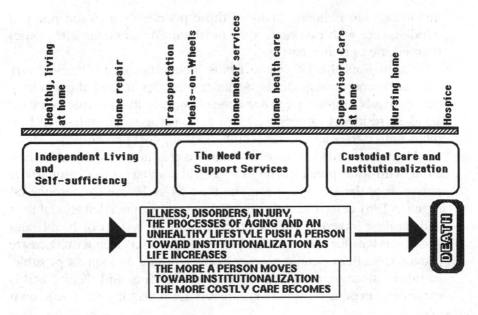

FIGURE 1.4. *Long-Term Care Continuum*

hospitals, nursing homes, life care centers, senior centers and other organizations developed specialized services for the elderly.

The Need for Health Promotion Services

In 1992, the United States spent more than 12.5 percent of its Gross National Product (GNP), or $800,000,000,000, to provide health care to persons who where sick or injured. The preponderance of illness and injuries can be prevented. Yet the health-care system and politicians in the United States spend money on treating crises and maladies after they occur instead of preventing them. Very little effort or money is directed toward promotion of health and prevention of disease and injury. This posture has to change because one of the best ways to curb runaway spending on health care is by preventing illness, disability, and injury.

Table 1.3 presents the number of vital events for California in 1990 as an example of selected health status indicators. These statistics represent some areas in which health promotion and illness prevention services can make a difference. The number of live births gives a frame of reference; the other eight items are areas that can be

TABLE 1.3. *Selected Vital Events for California, 2000*

Live births	531,285
Homicides	2,084
Heart disease	68,533
Cancer	53,005
Suicides	3,113
All accidents	8,814
Infant deaths	2,884
Fetal deaths	3,046
Maternal deaths	59

SOURCE: State of California, Department of Health Services Birth, Death, and Fetal Death records, 2002. Acknowledgment: Phillip Coon, Research Analyst Health Statistics, Riverside County Department of Public Health.

decreased through health promotion and disease and injury prevention. When these various factors are reduced, health status for citizens of California will improve. Similar results can be achieved nationwide.

In industrialized nations today, most diseases are directly associated with lifestyle and/or are behaviorally caused. Viewed by disease, the leading causes of death in the United States are presented in Figure 1.5. The top four causes of death are directly related to the behavior of individuals and comprise 75.6 percent of deaths in the United States; only 17.7 percent of deaths can be attributed to communicable diseases. Thus, health promotion and disease and injury prevention activities could substantially decrease unnecessary illness, disability, injury, and premature death. The top three actual causes of death in the United States are smoking, alcohol consumption, and poor nutrition/ diet (see Table 1.4).

Health and wellness factors and related risk factors are of two types: (1) those one *cannot* completely control and (2) those one *can* control (see Table 1.5). Basic to health promotion and overall well-being is the notion that each individual is responsible for his or her own health and behavior.

Health promotion and prevention activities aim to influence and change risk factors. As health promotion programs are proposed or considered for large industries, hospitals, local governments, and other organizations, initial health testing and screening activities are conducted. These assessments should identify specific health promotion services and programs to be developed to reduce the risks and

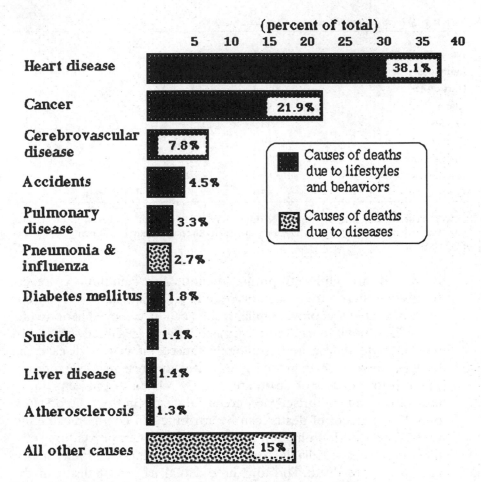

FIGURE 1.5. *Leading Causes of Death in the United States in 1991*

SOURCE: National Center for Health Statistics.

enhance the health of employees; this, in turn, reduces medical insurance cost, employee and employer health insurance premiums, and unnecessary use of health-care resources.

Services for Older People

The following is a fairly comprehensive list of services that could be developed in a community to help the aged remain at home, assure their independence by keeping them free from institutionalization, and maintain their dignity and life's savings. Table 1.6 is a list

TABLE 1.4. *Risk Factors that Contribute to the Leading Causes of Death in the United States*

Heart disease	Smoking, hypertension, high cholesterol, lack of exercise, diabetes mellitus, obesity, and stress
Cancer	Smoking, alcohol use, diet, environmental factors (carcinogens), and obesity
Stroke (CVA)	Hypertension, smoking, high cholesterol, stress, and lack of exercise
Accidents	Alcohol abuse; not using seat belts; lack of education; and lack of carefulness in work, recreation, and travel
Chronic obstructive pulmonary disease and lung diseases (COPD, COLD)	Smoking and air pollution
Diabetes mellitus	Obesity
Suicide	Stress, alcohol, and drug abuse
Cirrhosis	Alcohol abuse
Atherosclerosis	Smoking and high cholesterol

of historical health services, aging, and social service and planning events.[8-11]

Adult Day Care These centers are licensed community-based programs that provide nonmedical care to older persons in need of personal care services, supervision, or assistance to perform activities essential for daily living. This help is available at a drop-off center during the day.

Adult Day Health Care A community-based program provides medical, rehabilitative, and social services to elderly persons and other adults with functional impairments, either physical or mental, for the purpose of restoring and maintaining optimal capacity for self-care. These services are for persons at risk of being institutionalized and include individualized care plans.

Adult Social Day Care Licensed community-based programs provide nonmedical care to meet the daytime needs of individuals who are physically able to go to a local center. A plan of care in a structured comprehensive program provides a variety of social, psychosocial, and related support services in a protective setting.

TABLE 1.5. *Health Risk Factors*

One CANNOT Control

Heredity	Some genetic traits may make one susceptible to certain diseases.
Environment	Air pollution, water pollution, radiation exposure, chemical exposure are hazards to everyone.
Sex	Certain diseases affect only women or men, such as cervical cancer in females and prostate cancer in males.
Age	Of all the characteristics, age will show more difference in health status than any other variable. As one ages, resistance to disease diminishes and recovery slows.

One CAN Control

Exercise	Cardiovascular and respiratory fitness, muscle tone, weight control, stress relief are all benefits of an exercise program.
Nutrition and Diet	Proper nutrition through a well-selected diet improves health and controls weight.
Rest and Sleep	Good health requires 7 to 8 hours of sleep each night.
Tobacco Use	Avoiding or stopping the use of tobacco reduces risk of respiratory diseases.
Alcohol Use	Avoiding the use of alcohol is the best choice, because it affects liver and brain functioning, causes driving accidents and work-related accidents, cancer, suicide, and homicide.
Drug Use	Use of illicit drugs affects liver functioning, driving and work accidents, cancer, suicide, and homicide.
Stress Reduction and Management	Stress is responsible for and aggravates emotional and physical problems.
Attitude	A strong sense of well-being and an optimistic outlook contribute to physical and emotional health.
Lifestyle and Behaviors	Most people in the United States die from heart disease, cancer, stroke, and accidents—all have components preventable by changes in lifestyle and behaviors.

Alzheimer's Day Care Community-based programs serve persons with Alzheimer's disease or related dementia, particularly those in the moderate-to-severe stages, whose care needs and behavioral problems may make it difficult for the individual to participate in other programs.

TABLE 1.6. *Key Events in Planning and Program Development for Aging Services*

1935	Social Security Act was passed.
1946	Hospital Survey and Construction Act of 1946, also known as the Hill–Burton Act, was signed.
1954	Hill–Burton Act provided authority for grants to construct and equip nursing homes and related facilities.
1958	Small Business Administration authorized to provide loans to persons developing or building nursing homes as a small business enterprise.
1961	First White House Conference on Aging convenes.
1964	Community Action Programs were created by the Economic Opportunity Act to provide federal monies to establish social services and health programs for special populations, including many programs for the elderly.
1965	Medicare, Title 18 of the Social Security Act, was passed to provide medical insurance to those eligible for Social Security, mostly elderly persons. Title 18 also allowed payment of post-hospital care in long-term care facilities.
	Medicaid, Title 19 of the Social Security Act, was passed to provide hospitalization, physician care, tests and treatment, and nursing home care for those who qualified by meeting poverty guidelines, which included many elderly and nursing home patients.
	The Older Americans Act was passed to establish national policy concerning older Americans and provide monies for demonstration projects, research, planning, program development, implementation of services for the elderly, and special training programs in gerontology.
	Federal monies matched by state and local monies provide planning and development of health and social support services at the county and intrastate regional levels.
1965	The Heart Disease, Cancer, and Stroke Amendments of 1965 created the Regional Medical Programs to plan and develop a variety of health-related programs, many targeted at the elderly.
1966	Comprehensive Health Service Amendments Act (PL 89-749) laid the groundwork for health-planning programs, which also impacted health services for the elderly.
1967	Partnership for Health Amendments (PL 90-174) created the Comprehensive Health Planning (CHP) Agencies. The "A" agencies were administrative and conducted research for planning. The "B" agencies were developed at regional and county levels to conduct local need assessments, research, and planning. Much of the research from CHPs included services and programs used by elderly persons.
1968	Two levels of nursing home care and intermediate-care facilities were recognized as separate levels of care to qualify for participation in Medicaid payments.

TABLE 1.6. *Continued*

1969	White House Conference on Aging called for by President Nixon.
1971	Second White House Conference on Aging held.
1974	National Health Planning and Resources Development Act (PL 93-641), called Health System Agencies (HSA), was to control the addition of unnecessary hospital and nursing home beds, purchase of major equipment, and participation in health planning activities. Certificates of Need were required to build new nursing homes and hospitals or add beds to these facilities so growth would be planned and costs contained.
1973–1978	Amendments expanded to Older Americans Act and Social Security Act. Changes in mental health laws included the elderly, as did changes in nutrition services and health services laws to encourage home health care. A new major focus was placed on the frail and vulnerable elderly.
1986	Home System Agencies disbanded and the end of National Health Planning and Resources Development Act (PL 93-641).[8,9,10,11]

Case Management enables functionally impaired older persons to obtain services that promote and maintain their optimum level of functioning in the least restrictive setting. Services include assessment of psychosocial and health needs, development of plans for individualized care, arrangement of existing resources and services to meet the needs of the older person, and periodic monitoring of each client's care plan.

Congregate Dining Nutritious meals are served daily at centers where the elderly come to eat, socialize, and participate in nutrition education or other educational or recreational activities.

Consumer Assistance/Protection This service helps older persons avoid exploitation and assists in purchasing quality goods and services at lower costs. Some programs include discounts, consumer education, and assistance in financial matters and applications.

Employment/Second Career Counseling This service helps older adults secure appropriate employment opportunities. Special efforts are made to assist the older adult in selecting and entering a second career.

Friendly Visitors/Senior Companions A healthy person voluntarily develops a relationship with an older and somewhat disabled person and then visits this homebound person weekly or more often as agreed on by both parties. The volunteer visitor may just chat, help with household chores, or take the person to the store or doctor's office.

Health Education programs are targeted specifically at older adults. Topics of special interest are presented by medical or health education specialists to groups in senior centers and hospitals or through other avenues that can reach large populations of older persons.

Health Promotion for older adults can be any combination of health education, health screening, illness prevention programs, and organized interventions designed to facilitate behavioral and environmental adaptations for the older adult. These activities are designed to improve or protect the health of the elderly while improving their quality of life and well-being through increasing awareness and providing informed choices about maximizing health status.

Health Screening Brief examinations reveal a need for in-depth medical evaluation and referral. Collection of information about the older adult determines the need for a medical service and other recommendations to remedy the problem. Good health screening includes referral, evaluation, and follow-up.

Home-Delivered Meals (Meals-on-Wheels) Prepared hot meals are delivered to the homes of people who are unable to cook for themselves or who would be unable to maintain proper levels of functioning without the meals being brought to their homes.

Home Health Care Skilled and supportive nursing and medical services are provided to a person in his or her place of residence. Under the supervision of a physician, supportive nursing services, physical therapy, speech therapy, occupational therapy, pharmacy services, and any other needed services are provided for the ill, recovering, or disabled person at home.

Home Repair can be offered on an emergency basis or an ongoing basis as needed. This service often deals with an agency that has its own contractor's license and that works to protect the elderly while providing home repairs at reasonable prices.

Homemaker A person hired by an agency goes to the disabled or older person's home to perform housekeeping chores ranging from cleaning to preparation of meals.

Hospice Care provides specialized social, medical, and mental health support and care for terminally ill clients and their families. Services can be offered at home, in a nursing home, a hospital, or a separate freestanding hospice facility.

Housing Assistance This area consists of services designed to locate, maintain, improve, and reduce costs of housing for older persons by helping with placement, repairs, maintenance, renovation, reduced rent based on ability to pay, and so on.

In-Home Assistance These are services provided to elderly persons in their homes to assist in maintaining independent living or to provide respite for the family or caretakers. Services can include chores, housekeeping, homemaking, and personal care.

Legal Assistance Legal advice and counseling by attorneys and para-legals is offered to senior citizens at a central location or through visits to centers or other appropriate locations.

Medigap Counseling Counseling for the elderly helps them to better understand Medicare, Medicaid, private medical insurance, and nursing home insurance policies. A counselor reviews co-insurance and any other insurance the elderly may wish to purchase to ensure that they do not buy unnecessary policies and to identify areas Medicare and Medicaid do not cover.

Mental Health Psychological, psychiatric, and/or social work services improve and maintain the mental health of older persons through providing comprehensive assessments, therapy, referrals, education, and training as needed.

Ombudsman Ombudsmen work mostly with nursing home residents and are independent, objective, neutral persons who identify, explore, and resolve conflicts. Ombudsmen help with problems about quality of care, food, finances, meaningful activities, visitors of choice, residents' rights, and so on.

Respite Care This service consists of activities and services to support and provide relief for family or caregivers who provide substantially full-time care at home to frail or impaired older adults.

Security/Crime Prevention This service enhances the safety and security of older persons, reduces anxieties about crime, reduces chances of becoming a victim, and assists those who have been victimized. The program can include but is not limited to devices for security and safety, escort services, training in self-protection and security, and so on.

Senior Driver Education Two types of educational programs for older drivers have been developed. One is a preventive driving approach to reduce fears and sharpen driving skills. The second program is for senior citizens who have had one or more tickets or an accident and uses a defensive-driving/traffic-school approach to reduce risk of accidents and future tickets. Programs may be offered in a variety of settings such as senior and community centers.

Support Groups Organized meetings of persons with particular emotional needs share and discuss the problems the members face. The groups can be organized by retirement homes, hospitals, senior centers, churches, and community interest organizations.

Telephone Reassurance A healthy and self-sufficient person voluntarily calls a homebound or insecure person each day at the same time to check on his or her safety and well-being.

Transportation Vans or minibuses provide transportation for older adults or the handicapped to physicians, pharmacies, hospitals, clinics, senior citizen centers, churches, or stores.

Volunteer Programs Any organization operates more effectively and has an increased sense of community importance if an effective volunteer program is developed and operational. Programs with older adults as volunteers should provide meaningful work and have the minimum of a half-time paid director.

Program Development for Aging Services

Advances in public health, preventive medicine, health education, and medical technology over the past fifty to sixty years have caused great changes in the structure of the population of industrialized nations. Most Americans now live much longer than they did in 1900. The main causes of death in 1900 were pneumonia and upper respiratory diseases, tuberculosis, and other infectious diseases that were due to the uncontrolled spread of harmful bacteria and other pathogens (refer to Figure 1.5). Through public health measures, more and more people have lived to grow old. Major public health efforts that have changed disease patterns and life expectancy include cleaning up public water supplies; sanitation; preventive medicine programs, such as immunizations against communicable diseases; health education efforts, such as disseminating information on early childhood vaccination programs; and the development of and advances in medicine and drugs such as penicillin and other antibiotics. Through these measures and changes in lifestyles, developments in medical technology, and new surgical techniques and treatments, the fastest growing segment of the population is older adults.[13-17]

The over-65 age group continues to grow at such a rapid pace that it now makes up a major portion of the population of the United States. This group has been categorized in several ways. One older adult group is the "young-old"—the healthy, independent, and active group. A second group is the "old-old"—those who have lived into their late seventies and beyond, yet are fairly healthy, independent, and active. A third category of older persons is the "frail"—those vulnerable, ill, and at risk due to mental illness, chronic diseases, and/or disabilities.[10]

Program development administrators and planners for services aimed at the aged need to have a good understanding of the population. A review of the major demographics and population data of older Americans is an important and worthwhile task.

There has been a major change in the age distribution of the total population of the United States in recent years. Approximately 28 to 30 million Americans, about 12 percent of the population, are 65 years of age or older. The 75 years and older age group is now the fastest growing segment of the population in the United States. Women outnumber men in the 65 and older group. In 1984, there were 16.7 million older women and 11.3 million older men, or 148 women for every 100 men over age 65.[12,14] In 1983, whites made up 91.9 percent of the population over age 65, blacks were the second largest group at 7.7 percent, and Hispanics comprised 0.3 percent of the over-65 population. Asians and others made up the remaining 1 percent.[9] From 1950 to 1983, average life expectancy for women increased from 71.1 years to 78.1 years, an increase of 7.0 years. For the same period, men increased their average life span by 5.4 years from 65.6 years to 71 years.[13,14,15]

Some additional data and demographic facts about older Americans may be valuable to those who plan and develop programs for the aged. Older persons have less formal education than their younger counterparts. In 1984, the median number of school years completed by older people was 11.4 years. In 1988, approximately 9 percent of older adults had four or more years of college, compared to about 15 percent of the population having a bachelor's degree. About 24 percent of older persons are employed, with 11.6 percent of men and 4.2 percent of women over age 65 employed full-time, and 4.3 percent of men and 4.0 of women employed on a part-time basis.[13,16] The median income of older persons in 1984 was $10,450 for men and $5,200 for women. Older persons who live with nonrelatives or who live alone are more likely to have less money than those who live with family or in a multiperson household. The elderly make up a disproportionate amount of the poor in the United States, with 21 percent of those over age 65 living at or below the poverty level.[13,15,17]

Older people are more typical of the general population than some myths and misconceptions lead one to believe. Most of those over age 65, especially the "young-old," are the independent, active, and quite healthy grandmothers and grandfathers whom most people know but fail to categorize as elderly. Only 4 to 5 percent of the older population is in nursing homes. The average age of those in nursing homes is 82 to 85 years and most of these people have four to five chronic diseases and are quite ill. Actually 71 percent of older men live with their wives and an additional 7 percent live with children or relatives. As for the women, only 36 percent live with their husbands and 18 percent live with children or relatives. Of those who do live alone, most live close to family with whom they have frequent contact. Studies show that only 5 percent of older adults had no contact with family or friends within the previous two-week period.[14,16] Only 30 percent of the older population lives alone. Most older people are not socially isolated, yet many older adults suffer a great deal from loneliness. Some stay socially active—about 75 percent are members of a church or synagogue and more than 50 percent belong to volunteer organizations.[13-16]

The Need for Health and Social Services

Today, many programs and support services for the elderly are in place and functioning well. Many communities, however, still lack special programs to serve the needs of an aging population. As the number of people who reach old age increases, the need and demand for health care and social services for this population will increase. Concurrently, in some cases, federal and state financial support for health and social programs has decreased or been discontinued. As governmental programs do not keep up with the needs of the aged, hospitals and private health organizations develop services. Consequently, there is a need for the effective use of resources to ensure that these efforts are financially worthwhile. This requires effective and proven planning methods and approaches.[18]

As one studies the many planning, program development, and evaluation methods developed and used over the years, similarities in process, terminology, and techniques are readily observed. Some methods may be simpler than others. Techniques will vary from experience to experience and may have different approaches each time but the fundamentals remain the same.

The actual planning and program development process may not fall into place and be conducted as orderly as the steps in the model presented in this book. Planners may have some of the processes already in place or completed when the project is assigned or initiated. The person in charge of planning and program development needs to examine other processes and approaches and determine if the project at hand demands more precise information or additional specific intricate planning methodology. If so, the planner is encouraged to search out methods in other planning and administration books and manuals. The information in this book should not restrict the planner from using different approaches and methods, which may be appropriate to the situation or to the particular project to be developed, if more complex or new and innovative methods are required.

References

1. Bloch, A. *Murphy's Law: Book Two*. Los Angeles: Price/Stern/Sloan, 1981.
2. Timmreck, T. C. "Working Model of Patient-Health Education." *Radiologic Technology* 51, no. 5 (March/April 1980): 629–635.
3. Deeds, S. G. *The Health Education Specialist: A Self-Study Guide for Professional Competence*. Los Alamitos, CA: Loose Canon Publications, 1992.
4. O'Donnell, M. P. *Health Promotion in the Workplace*. New York: John C. Wiley, 1984.
5. Saunders, R. P. "What is Health Promotion?" *Health Education* 19, no. 5 (Oct./Nov. 1988): 14–18.

6. Timmreck,T. C., Cole, G. E., James, G., and Butterworth, D. D. "The Health Education and Health Promotion Movement: A Theoretical Jungle." *Health Education* 18, no. 5 (Oct./Nov. 1987): 24–28.

7. Deeds, S. G. *The Health Education Specialist: A Self-Study Guide for Professional Competence.* Los Alamitos, CA: Loose Canon Publications, 1992.

8. Rubinson, L. and Alles, W. F. *Health Education: Foundations for the Future.* Prospect Heights, IL: Waveland Press, 1984.

9. Spiegel, A. D. and Hyman, H. H. *Basic Health Planning.* Germantown, MD: Aspen Publishing, 1978.

10. Pegels, C. C. *Health Care and the Older Citizen.* Germantown, MD: Aspen Publishing, 1988.

11. Hyman, H. H. *Health Planning: A Systematic Approach.* Germantown, MD: Aspen Publishing, 1975.

12. McCenaghan, W. A. *American Government.* Newton, MA: Allyn and Bacon, 1985.

13. Office of Disease Prevention and Health Promotion, U.S. Public Health Service, U.S. Department of Health and Human Services. *Disease Prevention/Health Promotion: The Facts.* Palo Alto, CA: Bull Publishing Company, 1988.

14. Payne, B. P. "The Older Volunteer: Social Role Continuity and Development," *The Gerontologist* 17, no. 7 (July 1977): 356–360.

15. U.S. Bureau of Census. *Current Populations Reports,* 1985.

16. National Center for Health Statistics. *Health U.S.,* 1985.

17. AARP, *A Profile of Older Americans,* 1985. Washington, DC: American Association of Retired Persons, 1985.

18. Timmreck,T. C. *Study and Results of the Survey Conducted by the Cache County Independent Living Project* (Areawide Model Project). Logan, UT: CYN Publication, 1973.

Chapter 2

Begin at the Beginning: The Mission Statement

THE EINSTEIN EXTENSION OF PARKINSON'S LAW

A work project expands to fill the space available.

WETHERN'S LAW OF SUSPENDED JUDGMENT

Assumption is the mother of all screw-ups.

MURPHY'S LAW[1]

CHAPTER OBJECTIVES

The main purposes of this chapter are to:

1. Review the reasons that planning and program development fail.

2. Compare the definition of a mission statement with goals and objectives.

3. Explain the functions, components, and purposes of mission statements.

STEP 1

MISSION STATEMENT: General Idea or Main Purpose

- This is usually based on a general observation, an obvious seen need or interest, or a need assessment result.

Pitfalls to Avoid

Several reasons for the failure of planning and program development have been recognized and verified by experience. These pitfalls include:

1. Top-level management of the organization does not endorse the planning process. If top-level administrators fail to support the program development and planning process with adequate resources, materials, staff, and finances, then planning and implementation will fall short of expectations or even fail. Top-level management has to be committed philosophically and politically to the process of planning and program development, as well as to the project to be planned and implemented.

2. Planning and program development are not integrated into the total management system, the strategic plan, as well as the operational plan for the organization.[2]

3. Managers and/or planners do not understand different dimensions of planning (budget planning, operational planning, program development, strategic planning, management by objectives).[2,3]

4. Management personnel at all levels are not directly engaged in program development and evaluation. Often planning is delegated, thus removing managers from the process, the outcomes, and the responsibility.[2,3]

5. Responsibility for program development and planning is vested solely in a planning department, again removing managers from involvement in the process, the outcomes, and the responsibility.[2,3]

6. Too much is attempted at the same time or too many programs are planned at once.

7. Top administrators fail to recognize a fundamental premise of planning and program development; that is, plans are to be flexible and modified as things develop and the environment changes. In an ever-changing world, administrators mistakenly expect the plan to come true exactly as printed without allowing for change.[2,3,4]

8. Top administrators fail to operate the plan once it is complete, which may be due to not having been involved in the planning process in the beginning.[2,3,4]

9. Financial projections and budgeting are the sole criteria used. These are not sufficient bases for program development.[2,3]

10. Inadequate and limited information is used in the planning process. Good planning approaches require gathering all pertinent information.[2,3]

11. Emphasis is placed on one aspect of planning while ignoring the total program development and planning process, including the importance of the involvement of management.[2,3]

Definitions

A *mission statement* is a statement by an organization that contains detailed information about the overall direction and purpose of the organization. Additionally, it is an administrative statement that guides planning and decision making, and it is not restricted by any time element. A mission statement should contain the philosophy of the organization—specify the level and type of services provided, set forth the major functions of the organization, identify the service area or population and special formal and informal relationships with other organizations.[5]

A mission statement is not a goal per se; a goal is viewed differently in the planning and program development process. A goal has a specific function, a different definition from that of a mission statement and of an objective. It is important to distinguish these three constructs because each has a special role and function in the development of a plan.

A *goal*, as defined and used in health promotion, social and health services planning, is a statement of a quantifiable desired future state or condition. A goal differs from an objective because it lacks deadlines, is usually long range, is relatively broad in scope, and provides guidance for the establishment of objectives. Objectives are used for the attainment of goals and fulfillment of the mission statement.[5]

Goals are accomplished by activities. The tools used to describe the specific activities of the goals are objectives. One or several goals are needed to accomplish the mission statement. Many objectives may be needed to accomplish each goal.

An *objective*, as used in health promotion and in social and health services program development and planning, is any short-term, measurable, specific activity having a time limit or timeline for completion. Objectives are used to reach goals. They specify who, to what extent, under what conditions, by what standards, and within what time period certain activities are to be performed and completed.[5] Objectives outline the specific tasks essential to accomplish already determined goals.

Developing Mission Statements

The development of a sound and useful mission statement is the first major activity in the planning process. Each organization, public or private, should have a mission statement(s). Every project or service also can benefit from its own mission statement.[6] Organizations which embrace the planning process have much more success than organizations which do not. The mission statement is the first step in any planning activity.[5]

The mission statement establishes an identity for the organization that is more expansive than what one individual or small group can bring to the organization. It has to be an enduring vision of future direction and values, even as personnel changes. A well-developed mission statement helps to fill individual and organizational needs and sets goals to accomplish them, to participate in worthwhile work, to achieve recognition, to accomplish set tasks, to observe program success, to advance individuals personally and professionally, to move the organization forward, to assist subunits in advancement and growth, to meet and succeed over the competition, and to earn respect. Thus, the mission statement is a public declaration of organizational beliefs, values, aspirations, and position, and it sets an attitudinal posture aimed at success.[6]

Mission statements are wide in scope. Being directional in purpose, the mission statement allows consideration of a range of goals, objectives, and strategies. The statement should be broad enough to allow creative growth, expansion, and the consideration of new possibilities.[6]

Purpose and Function

A sound mission statement sets forth the basic purpose of the project or program and distinguishes it from other programs. The mission statement identifies the scope of the program and provides overall direction to the project, program, or service. Once set, it should be an enduring statement of purpose. This all-important general declaration sets forth the foundation for establishment of priorities, directions, goals, objectives, plans, and strategies and is basic to the formulation of activities and work assignments.[6]

Structure and Parts

The mission statement, being the most basic and visible part of the planning and program development process, is comprehensive and broad in scope. There are several key parts to a useful mission statement. They include:

- A statement of the key elements of the philosophy, values, and beliefs the program embraces.
- The identification of the self-concept of the organization/ program.
- A statement of commitment the organization has to growth, stability, and survival.

- The identification of general service and catchment areas and target populations and markets to be served.
- A statement of specific services and programs to be offered.
- A statement of the desired public image of the services or programs being developed and offered.[5]

Legitimacy and Tangibility

Health promotion, social, and health services have been accused of intangible missions, especially when prevention is mentioned. Most mission statements are broad, idealistic, and intangible. It is through the planning process, and by writing goals to support the mission statement and objectives to support the goals, that mission statements become tangible and meaningful. Accomplishments of an organization can be measured only against specific, clear, focused objectives and goals that fulfill the mission statement. Only when objectives have been spelled out in measurable activities can resources be allocated to accomplish the mission. One of the most common reasons for failure is the allocation of resources or lack of it. It is a truism that top managers sometimes fail to adequately fund and support a planning project or a new program or service. Excuses will never suffice, however, for the lack of proper planning and goal setting. Legitimacy of the planning process comes when top management gives verbal support and adequate resources.[7]

Legitimacy is best observed when the mission statement and the goals of the organization are accepted and embraced by employees and managers alike. Both entities are more likely to give support and cooperation, and both are vital to a program's success. If the mission statement and goals are not seen as legitimate by workers and administrators, however, support is likely to be incomplete. If the results of a plan are of questionable utility, managerial concerns and issues lead to empty discussions.

Often individual interpretations of organizational mission statements give rise to individual goals rather than organizational goals. When concrete objectives are lacking, other factors determine whether the mission statement is positively perceived. In organizations that serve the elderly, poor, or needy, it is easy for individual altruistic efforts to supplant the mission of the organization. Many health promotion, health care, and human service workers give much value to work for its own sake. In addition, financial grants can misdirect the mission statement when the goals of the newly funded program follow the funding source's demands instead of the organization's mission and goals. Thus, as part of the program development process, the mission statement and goals need to be accepted, understood, and supported by all levels of personnel in an organization. Mission statements and goals should be marketed well and communicated clearly to all parties who may support, work within, or have the potential to defeat the program development and planning process.

Public statements of support by top administrators help to have the mission statement embraced as being worthwhile.[7] It has been discussed in the management literature almost from the very beginning that health promotion programs, health services, or social services need a clear statement of *mission*, with a dynamic leader to articulate it.[8]

References

1. Bloch, A. *Murphy's Law: Book Two*. Los Angeles: Price/Stern/Sloan, 1981.
2. Ringbakk, K. A. "Why Planning Fails." *European Business* 29 (Sept. 1966): 15.
3. Hyman, H. H. *Basic Health Planning Methods*. Germantown, MD: Aspen Publishing, 1978.
4. Fayol, H. *General and Industrial Management*. London: Pitman Publishing Limited, 1949.
5. Timmreck, T. C. *Dictionary of Health Services Management*, 2d ed. Owings Mills, MD: National Health Publishing Co., 1987.
6. Pearce, J. A. and David, F. "Corporate Mission Statements: The Bottom Line." *Academy of Management EXECUTIVE* 1, no. 2 (1987): 109–116.
7. Numerof, R. E. *The Practice of Management for Health Care Professionals*. New York: AMACOM, 1982.
8. Selznick, P. *Leadership in Administration*. New York: Harper & Row, 1957.

Chapter 3

Organization and Community Assessment

FOX ON DECISIVENESS

1. *Decisiveness is not itself a virtue.*
2. *To decide not to decide is a decision. To fail to decide is a failure.*
3. *An important reason for an executive's existence is to make sensible exceptions to policy.*

MURPHY'S LAW[1]

CHAPTER OBJECTIVES

The main purposes of this chapter are to:

1. Review approaches to internal assessment of the organization.

2. Assess the administration's acceptance of the planning process and the development of the proposed project.

3. Review and assess organizational resources needed to develop the project.

4. Determine the availability of resources for the proposed project.

5. Review approaches to external assessment.

6. Assess the potential for acceptance of the planning process and the development of the proposed project in the external environment (the community).

7. Review and assess community resources needed to provide assistance for the project.

8. Determine the availability of community resources for the proposed project and the willingness of community members to support the project.

9. Review the legal aspects of developing and implementing new programs and projects including regulations, corporate policy, and licensure.

STEP 2

Complete: Assessment and Evaluation of Organization, Inventory of Resources, and Review of Regulations and Policies

Internal Assessment

- Does the organization have the ability and resources to do the project?

- Does anyone care if the project is done, i.e., administrators or elderly recipients?

External Assessment

- Will the community accept and support the project?

- What are the government regulations affecting the project?

- What are the legal issues?

- Are there any zoning considerations?

Resources

- Money and finances
- Building space
- Personnel
- Equipment and materials
- Transportation
- Expertise
- Motivation and commitment
- Management audit
- Support for:
  –Organization
  –Community/consumer
  –Employees
  –Board
- Plan for evaluation process

Regulations and Policies

- What are the governmental limitations, restrictions, barriers, and requirements?
- What are the policy limitations, restrictions, barriers, and requirements?

Wars are won, not on the battlefields,
but within the generals' tents.

Planning is the most fundamental, yet most important, administrative activity organizations can conduct. Formal research studies as well as informal observations show that those who plan and use basic planning methods are much more successful than those who do not. Effective and successful development of any project relies on planning. A clear definition of the mission statement, a good assessment of the external environment, a sound analysis of the internal strengths, and a clear reading of the level and direction of commitment of the organization are basic considerations.

Some references refer to the assessment of the internal and external environment as audits—internal audits and external audits. Whatever the terminology and approach used, the assessment of the organization's commitment to planning and program development has to be clear if programs are to succeed. Choosing a project and a path through which it can be developed is a fairly simple and straightforward task. However, when one considers the personal goals and aspirations of the administrator or an informal leader, combined with the politics, complications, quirks, and conditions found in an organization, it is clear that planning and program development may encounter difficulties. These variables must be acknowledged and dealt with if planning and program development activities are to succeed.

Does Anyone Care? or What Are the Political and Administrative Constraints to the Program Development Process?

One question the director of program development and planning should ask prior to going too far into the planning process is: "Does anyone care if this program is developed?" This question applies both internally and externally to the organization. If only the project initiator wants to do the project, maybe the project is not worth pursuing. If the administration of the organization is only moderately interested in the project, one has to ask: "What are the chances for success and for obtaining the resources needed to ensure success for the program?" Nothing is more disheartening to a committed program developer than putting extensive amounts of effort into planning and the promotion of a project only to arrive at implementation time to find that the administration is not all that interested. If the administration is not committed to a project, most likely they will not be willing to commit the resources necessary for its success.

To ascertain the administration's acceptance of the development of a proposed program, the planner must not only tune in to the direct and straightforward verbal commitments but be aware of the subtle hesitancies, conditions, and political messages of minimal commitment. An outright rejection of a proposed program is easy to accept; once it is known the project will not be accepted, one can move on to new projects and more productive activities. However, to be given a verbal go ahead from the administration of an organization even though these same administrators lack a firm commitment to the notion is most difficult to deal with. If one goes ahead, it is a waste of time and resources. To not go ahead may be seen as not doing one's job, not following orders, and not being successful in one's position.[2,3,4]

Failing to include an assessment of the internal and external commitment can make planning efforts a futile exercise. Implementation time may be when the planner finds out how much commitment the administration really had to the project. The end of the planning process is not the time to learn that administration is not that interested or that hesitancies exist. Implementation time is not the time to learn that resources for the project are not available. If this occurs, time, resources, and effort have been wasted; this lack of insight can occur if internal and external assessments have not been completed early in the planning process. The beginning of a project is the time to ascertain commitment and determine if resources are available.

Internal Assessment

An internal analysis should be conducted at the beginning of the planning process; it will show the current status of the internal affairs of the organization. Internal analysis allows one to determine how well the organization is accomplishing its mission and to see the organization's strengths and weaknesses. In turn, internal assessment allows insights into whether the organization has the wherewithal to accept and implement a new project. An organization wanting to develop a new service or program will have areas which are strong and areas where resources are sufficient; other areas may be found to lack resources and to be weak. Viewed from a management point of view, it is safest to identify the organization's weaknesses, strengths, and general ability to accept and successfully implement a new project.

Any internal assessment will provide a realistic organizational profile and should include trade-offs, value judgments, unclear decisions, and educated guesses as well as some clear-cut answers and objective analyses. The goal is to provide a systematic internal analysis of the organization. This process should present an objective organizational profile so realistic decisions and a clear direction can be provided.

There are many useful approaches to internal assessment of an organization. Some are quite complex—using accounting and quantitative methods—and thus are more effective in areas which lend themselves to and are more accepting of quantitative analysis. A few quantitative methods include, but are not limited to: "Multi-attribute Utilities, Utility Curves, Anchored Rating Scales, Decision Trees, etc."[5]

Some methods are more qualitative in nature and therefore are straightforward, quicker, and less scientific. Both quantitative and qualitative approaches have their merits and their limitations. Quantitative approaches may take longer and cost more money to accomplish yet can produce more concrete facts and more detailed results. However, they are difficult to obtain (unless the planner has training and skills in them) and are more complex and harder to quickly comprehend. Thus, many program development managers rely on less sophisticated qualitative models that can produce good enough information and answers at less cost and less time, while still providing valuable assessments. The more straightforward, less quantitative methods are presented here. Program development and planning questions also are discussed.

Resource Analysis

The process of internal analysis is not done on a regular basis in most organizations nor are data related to the process systematically kept for this purpose. Yet, internal analysis is critical to the success of program development, and the process of internal analysis is neither linear nor simple. The approaches or steps used by managers at different levels tend to overlap. Managers tend to utilize different items in the analysis. Various levels of management often want different kinds of information and collect data that is appropriate for use in their department and at their level. Consequently the information may be different from that needed by a program development manager or a planner.[3]

Strengths and Weaknesses

One simple and straightforward method of resource analysis is the strengths and weaknesses analysis. In the program development process, each resource area needs to be assessed for strengths and weaknesses. Several approaches can be used to accomplish this task. The program development manager could simply list them; however, this is a less effective way. Other approaches provide more objective results.

A brainstorming process—listing the strengths in most key managerial areas (suggested below) on a flip chart or blackboard by key administrators or key persons—could provide many more insights and provide more objective input. Focus groups have been most effective in strategic planning and would work well in program development as well. A Delphi Method also is effective. However it is done, the strengths and weaknesses need to be reviewed and, moreover, the internal ability to support the proposed project has to be addressed.[5,6]

Strength and Weakness Assessment Activity

One approach to assessing the organization's internal posture on an issue would be to conduct a group brainstorming type session. In this session the strengths and weaknesses would be listed on the board or a large paper pad, combined with a discussion of all possible causes of the weaknesses.

Money and Finances

A major barrier to the development of a program is the lack of funds or the lack of a willingness to commit funds. Additional constraints can include: the proposed project is not part of the formal budgeting process, the project is not considered as important in the competition for the limited funds of the organization. If the administration of an organization is willing to commit monies to a program and its development, this becomes a strong psychological and political message that the proposed project will be supported financially and politically. If only a small percentage of the money requested is provided, depending on the amount, the project director might reconsider the project's actual position and administrative support. At this point, the planner decides whether to move forward or consider ending the process or at least discussing the matter with administration.

PLANNING QUESTION

☐ Psychologically and politically, is the administration of the organization willing to commit adequate financial support and resources to ensure the success of the project currently being planned?

Space and Physical Facilities

Space needs and space constraints in the planning process depend on the scope and breadth of the project at hand. If you are opening an outpatient center for older adults, new or remodeled examining rooms, reception centers, physician offices, storage, and so on would be needed. If you start a health promotion project—health education for the elderly—temporary or occasional-use space, such as use of a teaching room, would be easily arranged from existing facilities with little or no additional space necessary except for offices and storage. If a transportation project for the elderly were to be developed, a different set of facilities would be needed such as dispatch office, program director, maintenance and storage garages, and so on. Some large organizations, especially hospitals with low occupancy rates, can absorb new projects into existing space that is empty. Most organizations have to account for use of the space and cost through either accounting or budgeting procedures. If outside grants are available, rents and leases can be written into the grant and the agency or organization can be paid for the use of rented space, or specialized space could be acquired.

The planner needs to be sure that adequate facilities are available for the proposed project. Adequately planned space and proper project space, especially for older or handicapped persons, is crucial. Handicapped inaccessibility—lack of wheelchair ramps, narrow doors, and improper rest room facilities—could be barriers to success of a project.

PLANNING QUESTIONS

☐ Psychologically and politically, is the administration of the organization willing to commit to adequate building space to ensure success of the project currently being planned?

☐ Are funds available for acquiring external space?

☐ Are there locations or spaces available outside the organization that can be used for free or by trade arrangements—such as providing health education for the elderly at a senior citizens' center with no space costs incurred and both groups benefit?

Personnel

In health promotion and health care and human services, personnel account for the majority of the financial expenses. Ideally, a hospital, agency, or organization would prefer a grant be written to include not only salaries but benefits and administrative costs. The administration of any organization wishing to develop a new project will most likely want to know upfront about personnel needs and demands and especially who is paying for the salaries and for the benefits that usually make up 28 to 35 percent of the personnel costs.

Because staffing of a project is one of the major financial constraints in planning a new project, the personnel needs have to be carefully planned and well thought through. Each staff position has to be carefully justified (see Work Flow in Chapter 10).

If a grant has been written and budgets are available for staffing, the financial constraints can be managed easily. However, if no outside funding is available for staffing the project, the organization will not only have to assess the staffing needs but be willing to commit to adequately staffing the project. Many times promises for staffing are made by administration up front, yet when the project is actually implemented the staffing levels promised are not there. Therefore, realistic discussions about the willingness of administration to fully staff and support the project should be conducted at the beginning of the planning of the project. (See Appendix A: Budget Outline.)

Some administrators change their minds at the final stages of planning and ask the project director to modify the project and do a scaled-down "pilot project." Pilot projects, as a test of the possibility of success, are not an unusual approach to program development. However, if a pilot project is to be used as an afterthought with scaled-down staffing, success is put at risk. If a pilot project is to be used, this should be the approach discussed and planned initially. A pilot project, if planned as the preferred approach and determined at the outset of planning, is a worthwhile approach to test a program. However, if a pilot project is used as a halfway approach due to the reluctance of administration to fully commit to it at the last minute, this is unacceptable.

It is not uncommon, in unfortunate cases that lack planning and commitment, for administration to attempt to borrow personnel from other departments on a half-time basis, including clerical and secretarial help. Again, this shows a reluctance to commit to the project.

On the surface, these shortcut approaches may seem to be good managerial decisions. Past experience, however, has shown that a last-minute pilot project using borrowed half-time or quarter-time staff is actually programming the project and its director for failure. To be successful, a full-time director and adequate staffing needs to be committed upfront in the early planning stages of any project.

PLANNING QUESTION

☐ Psychologically and politically, is the administration of the organization willing to commit to adequate staffing and personnel to ensure the success of the project currently being planned?

Transportation

Staff Transportation

Some small projects, conducted in-house, may have no transportation needs. Therefore, transportation is not an issue that needs to be addressed in all program development efforts. Other projects may require some personnel travel that can be solved simply by paying the staff persons mileage to use their own cars, at the going Internal Revenue Service rate. Offering an aerobic exercise program at an industrial site may require the instructor to travel to the plant. Some projects for the elderly involve getting older adults to a center or hospital to participate in a program. If the project requires transportation of large groups of older persons, the transportation issue becomes a major planning issue to be dealt with. Some organizations already have buses and vans; other organizations may have to set up a transportation component for the project.

System of Transportation

Transportation becomes complicated when vehicles need to be purchased, insurance obtained, maintenance conducted or contracts arranged and paid for, and drivers and dispatch personnel hired. The more a proposed project involves developing elaborate transportation programs and approaches, the more resistance administration usually shows to a project. Transportation generally is expensive and often does not make money for the organization. Insurance and maintenance are expensive, vehicle purchases and personnel also are expensive, and the chance for legal involvement (a lawsuit) is quite high. Therefore, most administrators, unless they can see real value to a transportation program, are reluctant to get involved.

PLANNING QUESTIONS

☐ Psychologically and politically, is the administration of the organization willing to commit to adequate levels of transportation support (i.e., paying mileage, allowing use of existing vehicles, or purchasing new vehicles) to ensure the success of the project currently being planned?

☐ Is the need for transportation profound and real and is the value of transportation for the project seen by administration?

Equipment and Materials

Most new projects require some general office supplies and related materials. Additionally, some new office equipment—typewriters, computers, copying machines, medical equipment, and general equipment—may be needed. Special projects require special equipment; health education for the elderly may require printing and mailing equipment. Insurance counseling may require subscriptions to newsletters and insurance company and government (Medicare and Medicaid) publications. Transportation may need radios and specialized vehicles. Health promotion will need medical testing and screening equipment, and so on. Sometimes equipment and materials may already be available at the organization. Additional equipment and materials may need to be supplied or purchased by the administration of the organization. Assistance from sponsors which manufacture medical testing and screening equipment may be sought to subsidize and support health promotion services. The cost for the equipment needs to be determined and included in the budget for the project. (See Appendix A: Budget Outline.)

PLANNING QUESTION

☐ Psychologically and politically, is the administration of the organization willing to commit to purchasing or supplying the adequate supplies, materials, and equipment necessary for proper functioning of the program to ensure the success of the project currently being planned?

Expertise

Many hospitals, health and social service agencies, and organizations have many highly educated, well-trained, and experienced personnel working in the confines of the organizations. These same organizations also may have an organizational history of working in many of the areas closely related to the projects the organization may wish to pursue. Therefore, much in-house expertise may exist already and can be tapped into. Many organizations fail to recognize the talent and expertise that exists within their staff. Most organizations suffer from the "prophet has no respect in his own country" dilemma; thus, an assessment of the organization's personnel would be a wise thing to do. Some personnel are looking for chances to advance themselves, to change the routine of their work, retrain in new areas, or have new experiences and personal growth.

It may be worthwhile for the organization to formally inventory their staff to identify the training, education, degrees and expertise, ambitions, and interests that exist in the organization. It is not unusual for lower to mid-level staff persons to go back to school, obtain advanced degrees and training, and not make a public statement about their experience, training, and expertise. Second, biases and preestablished negative perceptions of certain staff members or personnel may be blocks to recognizing highly talented and capable persons, who, if given the opportunity, may do very well in a new role.

The key issue is: Does the organization have the expertise to plan, develop, and implement the current project? If the answer is yes, it is a matter of identifying those persons who have the expertise and reassigning them to the project. Second, it is important to determine if those persons with the expertise are willing to make the move to a new and, maybe, less secure position.

If the organization lacks the expertise to move forward with a proposed project, how does it go about obtaining the expertise?

One obvious and common approach is to hire a person with the proper expertise to take charge of the project or a least certain phases. Another possibility is to hire a consultant with the needed expertise. The feasibility of using a consultant has to be compared to hiring a full-time person. Consultants are expensive and are there only for a short time period, but usually, they have no employee-related expenses and benefits and are very good at what they do. Consultants are only in the organization temporarily and plan to leave; therefore, they have less commitment to the project's success. Because they bring to the organization a "new eye's view," consultants can solve problems quickly and resolve issues without concern for political constraints. These highly trained experts move through the organization much more freely because less restriction is placed on them by organizational policy and politics.

PLANNING QUESTIONS

☐ Does the organization have the expertise to take on the proposed project, or is the proposed project beyond the realm of the organization and its expertise?

☐ Does the organization have the financial ability to obtain the expertise and is it a good idea to take on the expense of obtaining the expertise? If the organization does have the expertise, this becomes an asset.

If the organization lacks the needed expertise, these fundamental planning questions need to be asked:

☐ Psychologically and politically, is the administration of the organization willing to commit to obtaining the level of expertise necessary to ensure the success of the project currently being planned?

☐ Should a consultant be hired to plan the project?

☐ Should the organization hire its own planner/program development manager?

Motivation, Commitment, and Support

Programs being considered or a project someone in the organization thinks is a good idea may be received with great enthusiasm and acceptance or may be rejected outright. When projects are presented by mid-level managers and directors to top-level administration, mixed responses are expected. Either of these scenarios is easy to deal with. If accepted and supported, the project will go smoothly because it will have the moral commitment of administration. In turn, the administration will put resources into the project. If rejected, the project will not have to be planned; the program development director knows where he or she stands on the matter and can move on to more productive activities. However, if the project is verbally agreed on when presented to higher administration just to appease the manager with the idea, the project may not be fully supported, or if the program development director has to do a great deal of convincing to get the project approved, the project is probably doomed to problems.

Lack of total motivation, commitment, and support by higher administration means the project director will be struggling to get resources, staffing, space, equipment, and materials as administration questions the value of the project in the first place. A wise and concerned program development manager will discuss the issues of commitment, the honest intent of the administrator, and his or her motivation to see the project brought to implementation and success. A word of caution about such discussions: The project manager must use a great deal of finesse, sensitivity, and proper communication approaches in discussing issues of commitment to projects. Be cautious. Do not alienate the administrators in the process, shed negative light on the planning process or department, or present an air of lack of competence as a planner.

Pushing a top-level administrator to a commitment may result in a shallow commitment or a half-hearted agreement just to end the pressure for a commitment, something the program manager may not want. Decisions to go ahead or to not proceed with a project need to be made early on. Once resources, time, and political commitment to a project have been made, it is difficult to back down or stop the process. If the organization has a board of directors and the board approves a project, it is even more difficult to halt the process of program development and planning. If a project is backed by board approval, it has a greater chance for success and for the commitment of resources by administration. Thus, to be effective in the program development and planning process, the motivation and commitment of the organization and its administration must be ascertained, understood, and discussed up front.

PLANNING QUESTION

☐ Is the administration of the organization motivated and committed psychologically and politically at the level necessary to ensure the success of the project currently being planned?

Management Audits

Management audit incorporates many of the items presented above. Still, it is worthwhile to present the basics of a management audit, as it is a useful tool for the internal assessment of the organization. The basics of a management audit are broad in scope and the audit includes each of the important operational parts of the organization. However, one specific management audit profile may not be appropriate for use in every instance. Each new circumstance requires the development of a new and separate management audit.

The following basic procedures used in conducting a management audit are general in nature. First one must review the overall efficiency and effectiveness of the administration of the organization. Nolan suggests looking at these four aspects:

1. *Development of Objectives.* Top-level management must develop formal objectives and the lower levels of management throughout the organization also must develop objectives, short-term and long-term.

2. *Review of the Current Planning Process.* Once objectives are developed and reviewed, the current planning process needs to be assessed. The items in the planning process should include: policies, procedures, schedules, and priorities that are used to carry out the operation of the organization.

3. *Assessing the Organizational Structure and Processes.* This step assesses the organizational structure and its internal processes to determine if they are in line with the overall objectives of the organization. Organizational structure must be able to accommodate objectives, goals, and the overall mission of the organization. In many instances, policies impede the development of programs or the healthy

functioning of an organization. Policies need to be assessed for effectiveness and usefulness.

4. *Assessment of Administrative Control.* Administrative controls ensure that the tasks and work activities that are supposed to take place actually do take place—moreover, that the tasks and work activities are in line with objectives, goals, missions, and the organization's plan. Three administrative control areas need to be ascertained: 1) the administrative areas that need control and how much, 2) the basis for which standards of assessment are to be determined, and 3) the criteria by which established performance and results will be measured.[7]

An approach to the above-mentioned management audit is presented in Table 3.1. The table is a skeleton outline and does not set forth all parameters, issues, and factors that need to be assessed. This outline merely provides a structure that may be useful to follow. It is based on the four elements discussed above.

Once the results of the management audit have been gathered, they need to be turned into a meaningful dialogue; the findings are in need of analysis. A thorough evaluation of the results helps to uncover problems. The analysis has to avoid accepting ineffectual management, policies, and procedures. If the analysis is stifled by fear of political reprisal, the management audit and the entire process and purpose have failed. An atmosphere of growth and development of the organization must come from the administrative team offering safety in the audit assessment process. The organization and its administrative team must be willing to risk objective critical reviews and findings for it to be a successful management audit.

A checklist form can be used to help solve management problems. A short example of how to structure the checklist is shown in Table 3.2. The management audit is an effective tool for internal assessment of organizations that are in the process of program planning, development, and implementation of new services.

Internal assessment of the organization is an essential step to be taken in program development and planning in order to not waste time and resources. If the organization does not have the wherewithal or the commitment to accept or initiate a project, the internal assessment will uncover the limitations. The organization's inability to move forward on a project will be discovered and the project should not be taken on. It is a poor approach to the program development and

TABLE 3.1. *Management Audit Program*

Management review process	Comments and solutions
Development of Objectives	
a) Assess all organizational objectives for last five years.	
b) Compare work and task results with objectives and goals.	Set realistic goals. Objectives must be measurable and within the mission of the organization.
c) Why did the organization not meet certain goals?	What were the barriers to and restrictions that kept the objectives from being met?
d) Etc.	Etc.
e) Etc.	Etc.
Review of the Current Planning Process	
a) Is there a master plan? Is this a useful plan? Is it being used? Is it a true Plan of Action, or merely a document for show?	The master plan is developed by a consultant, is not reviewed by administration, and is not used effectively.
b) Etc.	Etc.
Assessing the Organizational Structure and Processes	
a) Are the key administrators effective in their position?	Position titles and roles needed to be evaluated.
b) Is the organizational chart readable? Does it clearly show lines of authority and communication? Are positions and titles clearly set forth?	Organizational chart needs to spell out lines of communication better.
c) Etc.	Etc.
Assessment of Administrative Control	
a) Does the organization have adequate control over operations?	Many areas of control are too restrictive and inefficient.
b) Do policies, procedures, forms, filing systems work well?	Filing and forms need to be redone.
c) Etc.	Etc.

TABLE 3.2. *Management Audit Control List*

Area of problem: List of findings and problems	Comments: What has been done to remedy the problem?	Date
Administrative Control		
1. Policy and procedures limit development of new programs	Revision of policy/procedures completed with input from director of program development	10/9/01
2. Etc.	Etc.	Etc.
3. Etc.	Etc.	Etc.

planning process to wait until a great deal of time, effort, money, and other resources have been committed to a plan to find out that the organization or agency cannot take on the project. Internal assessment is as fundamental to the planning process as all other parts of the model.

External Assessment

The assessment of the external environment—the community—is based on premises similar to those found in marketing. It is of little value for a hospital, organization, or agency to set out to develop a service or program that the target group, such as the older adult population or the community, has no interest in. It is crucial, therefore, to determine the interest in and acceptance by the community of a proposed project. Assessment of the external environment can be as simple as interviewing a few of the possible participants, or as complex as trying to forecast demographic trends and economic implications for the target population. The program development manager needs to assess all environmental and community systems to identify barriers and constraints to development of the program as well as identifying opportunities. The manager not only must be interested in current opportunities, barriers, and constraints, but must look ahead to try to identify any future opportunities, barriers, or constraints. At this point in the program development and planning process, forecasting and planning are key roles for the program development manager.

The program development manager must use every available information source and technique to forecast future conditions. Some sources may include obtaining data and statistics that apply to the project from the county public health department or the state department of health services on health-related statistics. The county or regional office on aging (Area Agency on Aging) or the state office on aging also may provide current statistics and data. Local newspapers and the chamber of commerce also can provide data on the economic, industrial, social, demographic, and related data for a community, just to mention a few.[2]

The type and extent of program development will dictate the amount of time a person devotes to management. Some small projects may warrant only a part-time manager. Large projects should have a full-time manager at the minimum and maybe an assistant or two. Factors such as the size of the project, the degree of innovation and creativity put into it, the newness of the idea to the area, the target population, and the competition for the service will impact on the role of the project manager.

The concept of community analysis has several meanings. Dignan and Carr suggest analyzing every facet of the community from business and commerce to social and political structure to the organization and delivery of health services.[8] MacStravic suggests monitoring the constant changes in the economic environment of the community.[6] In health promotion planning for the community, Green and Kreuter suggest using the PRECEDE–PROCEED model for community diagnosis to assess the educational, behavioral, epidemiological, and social areas. Administrative and organizational diagnosis also are suggested (see Chapter 5).[9] If a major project, such as building a hospital or life care retirement center, is initiated, all facets and variables in the community that could change, influence, and impact the undertaking should be constantly watched.

Community assessment is a great learning process. It brings to light many aspects and various facets of the community that the organization may not have previously looked at and presents information from a different point of view. As one assesses the community, it helps the program development manager come closer to a complete understanding of the target population—the people, cultures, and environments—to be served.

The community has to be defined by its dimensions and boundaries. It is a group of individuals with common characteristics such as income, church affiliation, ethnic background, culture, race, and geographic boundaries. The community also can be the particular group or target population that is being served—the elderly community—or the workers of an industry that are to receive a comprehensive health promotion program.

Webber describes two basic types of interactions in the community: "place" and "non-place" activities. Place refers to those activities that occur in a particular geographic location and are most common to everyday activity. Non-place interactions are less obvious and extend to geographic locations beyond the neighborhood or geographically identified community. Services and health care often move older adults out of their place community into the non-place environments. The elderly and people in general are less comfortable in the non-place environment and prefer to return to familiar surroundings.[10]

If a comprehensive community analysis has not been done and the program development manager desires a complete, full-blown community analysis, the variables and factors shown in Table 3.3 should be looked at.[11]

The primary purpose of the external assessment of the community and environment is to ascertain support for a project. The specifics and fine details of community analysis will surface in Step 4 (Chapter 5) as the need assessment processes will provide the opinion and interests of the target population and the catchment area.

By speaking to community leaders, agency heads, public health and health promotional professionals, social service personnel,

TABLE 3.3. *Variables and Factors to Assess in a Community Analysis*

Seasonal variations	Climate
Location issues	Topography
Business and commerce	Demographic characteristics
Migration	Educational levels
Ethnicity	Income
Race distribution	Government structure and services
Community health status	Health care delivery system/services
Government social services	Nongovernmental support services
Church and community groups	Transportation
Economic centers/hubs	Health care centers/hubs
Catchment area determination	Target group/population

From Hochstrasser, Trapp, and Dockal (1968).

health-care delivery personnel, and selected potential recipients of the service in the community, an educated forecast of interest can be obtained. A visit to the local senior citizen center may produce interesting opinions on the needs of older people. An interview with the local hospital discharge planner and/or director of hospital social services provides insights into the service needs of sick or disabled persons. A visit with public health nurses and a visit with the director of the local office on aging will provide invaluable information about whether a proposed project or service for the elderly is needed. Health education and preventive medicine professionals in health maintenance organizations and public health departments and universities can offer insights into health promotion needs in a community.

Community Assessment

Assessment is the process of becoming familiar with the community. The community is a whole entity which has interdependence among its various parts. A community is made up of eight different subsystems surrounding the community core, which is made up of the people in the community. Although there is some crossover between the various areas, the boundaries between the areas are fluid and reflect the dynamic interrelationships with the whole community.

The first step is to acquire the core community data, which includes population, birth rate, death rate, unemployment, personal income levels, number of people living in poverty, total number of households, homeownership, renters, number of retired persons, number of persons receiving social security (and, for rural areas, the number of persons on farms).

There are eight areas of assessment. Details of each of these areas are presented next.

Physical Environment: This section includes terrain and weather—an assessment of the roads (snow removal, freeways, secondary roads), average annual temperature, rainfall, snowfall, and relative humidity.

Education: The number of elementary, middle school/junior high, secondary, and colleges/universities. Educational status is determined by the numbers of high school graduates and college graduates from both community colleges and four year colleges. Drug and alcohol use, tobacco use (both chewing tobacco and smoking), and violence statistics are to be included here. Number of teenage pregnancies could also be included in this section.

Safety and Transportation: This section includes fire protection (number of fire stations), police protection, number of police officers on the police force, and numbers of police cars, police motorcycles, and reserve officers. The most frequent crimes are to be listed as well as the services provided by the police. Public health and sanitation, including the water supply, sewage treatment, solid waste management, air quality, public health education, and restaurant and swimming pool inspections, should be included. Animal control processes should also be included. The primary means of transportation and numbers of public conveyances should be listed. The emergency medical system and the 911 system should be noted.

Politics and Government: The government structure for both city (include all cities and towns in the area if rural assessment) and county should be presented and assessed. The planning processes used by the government should be assessed. Councils of Government should also be included.

Health and Social Services: This section includes all hospitals, nursing homes, home health agencies, freestanding emergency centers, urgent care centers, industrial walk-in medical centers, outpatient facilities, emergency medical systems, mental health centers, aging services, adult protective services, child protective services, and all other social and health services.

Economics: This includes wealth or lack of it. The levels of income should be assessed. The number of people living below poverty level should be noted. Census data in relationship to labor force characteristics should be assessed. The number of persons working in heavy industry, light industry, service industry, government, trades, construction, utilities, transportation, financial services, etc., should be evaluated. Unemployment level should also be determined. Cost of living should be assessed and the impact it has on the working poor/medically indigent.

Communication: Communication can be informal or formal. Formal communication is in the form of media, newspaper, television, magazines, radio, and the Internet. Informal communication is in the form of bulletin boards, or posters placed on telephone poles at intersections of roads, tacked on buildings, and delivered to one's front door. Announcements in civic club meetings and in church are also another means of informal communication. Newsletters put out by civic organizations and churches are an informal communication process. Another informal part of communication is of people visiting one with another, in some instances this could be the negative form of chat that includes gossip.

Recreation: The number of recreation facilities and programs are to be listed, including Little League baseball, soccer, and football. City league adult baseball and soccer programs should be included. Swimming facilities and commercial recreational centers should be included in the assessment. The number of senior citizen centers should be noted. The number of lakes and/or rivers that are used for recreation should be included. Bike paths and jogging trails are a part of the assessment.

Because the model is divided into several areas of assessment, this provides the opportunity to have the work load divided up between several members of the planning team. Strengths and areas of concern can be easily identified and developed. Some areas can be divided into subcomponents for easy assessment, thus guiding the information gathering process.

This section was adapted from Anderson, Elizabeth T., and McFarlane, Judith M., *Community as Partner: Theory and Practice in Nursing.* Philadelphia: Lippincott-Raven Publishers, 1996.

PLANNING QUESTIONS

Two key program development and planning questions need to be asked again, but this time from a community perspective:

☐ Does anyone in the community care if the project is developed and implemented?

☐ Is there enough interest and concern to support the project once implemented?

Approaches to Acceptance of a Project

Through cost shifting some organizations may support a certain project if they believe it supports the mission of the organization. A hospital may develop and financially support a "Community Health Education for the Elderly" project. Such projects may be seen as part of the patient recruitment, marketing, and public relations objectives of the hospital.

If the organization is not willing to fund the project, the planner might ask: "What are the kinds and sources of revenue available in the community? From participants? Will there be enough participants or fees to pay for the program?"

Barriers to program or project acceptance within the community need to be determined and analyzed and their impact determined. Barriers to acceptance and support need to be identified, assessed, and analyzed to determine if the barriers or resistance are great enough in number and magnitude to cause the project to fail. The type and source of the resistance and barriers need to be assessed. Some barriers are easily overcome with education and communication. Other barriers are so major that the end result is that the project would not be accepted or supported and the effort would be in vain. Good public relations, marketing, community education, and communication with the target population usually remove most resistance and barriers.

PLANNING QUESTIONS

☐ Is the community interested, motivated, and committed psychologically and politically to the level necessary to ensure the success of the project currently being planned?

☐ And second: Is the community supportive and accepting enough to ensure the success of the project currently being planned?

Planning for the Evaluation Process

Management and planners need to plan for ongoing evaluation of the planning process and for upgrading the effective and efficient delivery of services. Quality programs can be assured only if an evaluation system is considered and in place. Consideration of the evaluation process must be done at the beginning of a project. As goals and objectives are developed and written, the planner should be anticipating the end of the project. The use of the goals and objectives should be a major part of the evaluation process. Evaluation should be a part of each phase of the project, needs to be conducted at the end of implementation of the project, and should be an ongoing process and a regular part of the management of the project once the program is up and running. Short-term outcomes or *impact evaluation* should be conducted on a routine basis. Long-term goals or *outcome evaluation* also should be in place to assess the effect on social and health status/epidemiological outcomes.

Policies and Regulations

Many organizations develop one-year, five-year, and ten-year plans. If an organization uses long-range planning approaches, every effort should be made to ensure that new projects and programs fall within the scope of the long-range or strategic plans. An organization should have only one overall master plan, and it must utilize the master plan. If the program development manager develops programs and projects without coordinating them with the master plan, the head of the organizational horse will be going one direction and the program development leg will be heading in another direction, defeating the mission and strategic plan of the organization. Organization policy should be established that requires only one strategic plan and that all program development plans stay within the strategic plan, within the mission statement and goals of the organization, all being unified in one overall direction.[12]

Many projects, though well planned and ready for implementation, never get off of the ground because the program development manager fails to meet the regulations and policies set forth by a whole array of government agencies. Regulatory agencies control various facets of organizations, programs, and services. Some of the regulatory agencies are located at the city level, some are run by county government, some are state-level agencies, and others are federal mandate. Table 3.4 is a selected list of the areas controlled by regulatory agencies.[12,13]

The program development manager needs to become acquainted with the regulatory agencies, their rules and regulations, and the personnel who administer the compliance assessments that affect the

TABLE 3.4. *Selected List of the Areas Controlled by Regulatory Agencies*

Fire and safety codes	Environmental health
Building and zoning	Public health and sanitation
Ombudsman issues	Licensure of business
Public guardian	Medicaid requirements
Business name registration	Health facilities licensure
Medicare requirements	U.S. Department of Justice (Drugs)
Special health and social services licensure	Pharmacy board/agency
Licensure of professional staffs	Affirmative Action issues
Labor unions	JCAHO
Boards of labor	Immigration and Naturalization Service
Occupational health and safety standards	

proposed project. In addition, the project director must become familiar with the various regulations and policies to ensure compliance and avoid unnecessary delays for lack of compliance. A copy of the regulations from each agency and regulatory body not only should be on hand but should be understood so compliance with the regulations can be accomplished easily.

References

1. Bloch, A. *Murphy's Law Book Three.* Los Angeles, CA: Price/Stern/ Sloan, 1982.
2. Virga, P. H. (Ed.) *The NMA Handbook for Managers.* Englewood Cliffs, NJ: Prentice-Hall, 1987.
3. Pearce, J. A. and Robinson, R. B., Jr. *Strategic Management*, 3d ed. Homewood, IL: Irwin, 1988.
4. Cone, P. R., Phillips, H. R., and Saliba, S. J. *Strategic Resource Management,* 1. Berrien Springs, MI: Andrews University Press, 1986.
5. Nutt, P. C. *Planning Methods for Health and Related Organizations.* New York: Wiley, 1984.
6. MacStravic, R.E.S. *Marketing by Objectives for Hospitals.* Rockville, MD: Aspen Publishing, 1980.
7. Nolan, J. *Management Audit.* Radnor, PA: Chilton Book Co., 1984.
8. Dignan, M. B. and Carr, P. A. *Introduction to Program Planning: A Basic Text for Community Health Education.* Philadelphia: Lea & Febiger, 1981.

9. Green, L. W. and Kreuter, M. W. *Health Promotion Planning: An Educational and Environmental Approach.* Mountain View, CA: Mayfield Publishing, 1991.

10. Webber, M. M. "The Urban Place and the Non-Place Urban Realm." In *Explorations into Urban Structures.* Philadelphia: University of Pennsylvania Press, 1964.

11. Hochstrasser, D. L., Trapp, J. W., and Dockal, N. "Community health study outline." In Dignan, M. B. and Carr, P. A. *Introduction to Program Planning: A Basic Text for Community Health Education.* Philadelphia: Lea & Febiger, 1981.

12. Fayol, H. "Planning." In *General and Industrial Management.* London: Pitman Publishing Limited, 1949.

13. Furukawa, C. and Shomaker, D. *Community Health Services for the Aged.* Rockville, MD: Aspen Publishing, 1982.

Chapter 4

Writing Goals and Objectives

SEAY'S LAW

Nothing ever comes out as planned.

HOWE'S LAW

Everyone has a scheme that will not work.

Murphy's Law[1]

CHAPTER OBJECTIVES—PART I

The main purposes of Part I of this chapter are to:

1. Explain the role of objectives in developing need assessments.

2. Present planning questions for need assessment development.

3. Define the terms *goals* and *objectives*.

4. Explain the differences between mission statements and goals.

5. Define and explain the differences between goals and objectives.

6. Explain the different types and levels of objectives.

7. Explain how to write goals and objectives and give examples for use in need assessments.

8. Provide key terms that are useful in writing objectives.

9. Review some pitfalls and shortcomings in writing objectives.

STEP 3

Write Goals and Objectives

- For need assessments and feasibility studies

Plan the work and work the plan.

PART I—Writing Goals and Objectives for Need Assessments

Why Develop Objectives for Need Assessments?

The role, function, and purpose of need assessments is presented in Chapter 5. How to plan for the need assessment and how to write goals and objectives are discussed in this chapter. Basic principles and philosophy of planning apply, in a limited way, to the need assessment development process. That is, planning a need assessment is basically the same as planning a new program or service. The fundamentals of planning are as applicable to the development of a need assessment as they are to any other endeavor.

Fundamental to the planning process is the writing of objectives. The development and writing of goals and objectives forces one to clearly think through what needs to be done and how to put needed activities into action. Failure to write goals and objectives, or using vague and general ideas of what is to be done, does not allow one to see the entire picture clearly. Without goals and objectives the planner can become sidetracked or fail to consider all the necessary factors. The actual writing of goals and objectives in itself is an excellent planning tool and should be taken seriously and done thoroughly. The valuable part of writing objectives is that it helps one determine every activity that needs to be completed, to what extent, under what conditions, and under what timeline each is to be accomplished.

This chapter is presented at this point in the model and the book because objectives need to be written for need assessment activities. The planner should clearly understand how to write effective objectives in order to develop need assessments and conduct this phase of the planning process. The major area for which overall planning goals and planning objectives need to be developed is presented just prior to the step-by-step activities in the planning process where specific activities are set forth. For the sake of continuity in subject matter, the section on writing program planning goals and objectives is presented in Part II of this chapter. Objective writing is one of the key tools of a planner and should be used in different phases of the planning process as appropriate. Once gaps in service and priorities are determined, implementation and program goals and objectives will be needed to effectively plan necessary services and activities as shown in Step 7.

PLANNING QUESTIONS

Objectives written in a clear and effective manner provide direction and understanding of those activities that need to be completed to develop a need assessment. Questions, which objective writing can answer, could include:

☐ What are the overall goals of the need assessment?

☐ What needs to be planned using the need assessment, and what can objectives be written for?

☐ What specific needs are to be addressed or ascertained that objectives can be written for?

☐   What are five to ten general areas that the need assessment is to cover?

☐   What type of need assessment is appropriate for the project at hand?

☐   What specific activities need to considered and included?

☐   What activities and objectives need to be accomplished in developing the need assessment form?

☐   What specific items or issues need to be included in the need assessment form or process?

Defining Goals and Objectives

Basic information on mission statements was presented in Chapter 2. Briefly a mission statement is a generalized future goal statement that contains information to provide long-term direction and purpose to an organization. A mission statement is to provide overall organizational direction and serves as a guide for future planning and decision making; it is a philosophical statement of the purpose of an organization. Therefore, it serves the planner with direction to ensure that need assessment development is in line with the overall direction of the organization. A mission statement is not included in the actual need assessment development. It is referred to in the planning process and the need assessment procedures, as it is a guide to the overall organization's philosophical direction. The mission statement serves to make sure new programs are meeting the strategic direction of the organization.[2]

Some Concepts about Goal and Objective Writing

Training and education on goal and objective writing have been a part of management by objectives, health planning, social services planning, grantsmanship, and related activities for a long time. Over the years, consultants and trainers have given their own twist to the goal and objective writing process in order to make the process more effective or to make their approach unique. Sub-goals, sub-objectives, methods versus outcomes, objectives outcomes, activities, sub-activities, and a variety of other terms often are used to give a more specific format to goal and objective writing just to be different. This book takes a more simple, yet fundamental, approach to goal and objective development to avoid embracing one certain approach.

Goals

In health promotion, health care and social services planning, a *goal* is defined as a quantified statement of a desired future state or condition. Goals are long-term hopes and aspirations. A goal should be a broad statement that is not directly measurable but is attainable. A goal differs from an objective in lacking a deadline, and usually they are long-range rather than short-term.[2,3]

Objectives

An *objective* is defined as any statement of short-term, measurable, specific activity having a specific time limit or timeline for completion. Objectives directly address the completion of the programs and state the expected result, the measurement to be used, and the time period in which to accomplish the result. Objectives have to be measurable and are used to reach goals. Objectives are quantifiable statements written out to specify who, to what extent, under what conditions or level of performance, or by what standards specific activities are to occur and what outcomes are expected. Each written objective states a specific time period by which certain activities are to be performed or completed. Each separate objective should be the partial accomplishment of a goal.

Objectives are phases of activities through which one should pass on the way to accomplishing a goal. Because goals are general and vague, objectives are specific statements detailing the activities needed to reach the goals and outcomes expected. Objectives need to be in line with goals. They should not be loosely connected to the goal, but should be directly connected to accomplishing it.[2,4,5] Goals should be in line with and accomplish the mission statement of the organization. All three factors should assist in fulfilling the strategic plan of the organization.

Objectives need to be written clearly. They should be action oriented, measurable, and detail the specifics of the goal. Use the KISS (Keep It Short and Simple) method when writing and developing objectives.[6] Usually several goals are written for each project.

Because objectives detail the activities and results of goals, several objectives generally are written to meet one goal.

Objectives: Levels and Types.   Some program planning and program development professionals prefer to break objectives down into two or three different types. Other planners suggest using decision trees to establish objectives—objective trees. In a decision tree (see Decision Trees in Chapter 5), all branches of the tree are specified by an objective, and lower-level objectives are used to contribute to and achieve higher-level objectives. All levels should have outcomes to be accomplished through stated activities. Some approaches suggest assigning individual responsibilities for certain activities and results.[7]

Objective levels have been developed and used by a variety of organizations, consultants, and trainers. One approach uses "higher-than-low objectives and low-level objectives." Another approach has three levels of objectives—high, intermediate, and low-level. Generally when objectives are broken down into levels, this means the lower-level objectives are aimed at the most detailed and most specific activities needed to accomplish the higher objectives—the overall objectives and goals. Other terms which have been used to describe the lower-level objectives, may include action objectives, activity objectives, sub-objectives, activity-directed objectives, short-term objectives, and so on.

A common approach one often encounters is to use the terms *general objectives* and *performance objectives*. The objectives that are developed are one of these two types. The general objective provides broad guidelines and direction to help make plans for accomplishing the goal. The performance objectives are more specific and measurable, and they state what is expected (outcomes) when and what is to be done.[10] One limitation to this approach is that it becomes confusing. It is difficult to separate out which is the goal and which is the general objective. When performance objectives are to provide specific and measurable aspects of the objective, the general objective basically is a goal instead of a true objective.

When conducting planning, government agencies use a three-phase or three-step approach. First, at the top of each page of the plan, they present the goal. Second, the objective, which states expected results, time factors, and conditions, is presented. The third part occupies the rest of the page. Action Steps, which are used to

```
┌─────────────────────────────────────────────────────────────────┐
│  GOAL 1.1                                                         │
│                                                                   │
├─────────────────────────────────────────────────────────────────┤
│  OBJECTIVE 1.1                                                    │
│                                                                   │
├──────────────────────────────────────────────────┬──────────────┤
│                                                    │   Date       │
│                  ACTION STEPS                      │   Due        │
├──────────────────────────────────────────────────┼──────────────┤
│ 1                                                  │              │
├──────────────────────────────────────────────────┼──────────────┤
│ 2                                                  │              │
├──────────────────────────────────────────────────┼──────────────┤
│ 3                                                  │              │
├──────────────────────────────────────────────────┼──────────────┤
│ 4                                                  │              │
├──────────────────────────────────────────────────┼──────────────┤
│ 5                                                  │              │
├──────────────────────────────────────────────────┼──────────────┤
│ 6                                                  │              │
├──────────────────────────────────────────────────┼──────────────┤
│ 7                                                  │              │
└──────────────────────────────────────────────────┴──────────────┘
```

FIGURE 4.1. *Example of Planning Sheets for Objectives and Action Steps*

meet the objective, are presented in numerical fashion. A column on the right lists due dates for each Action Step. One, two, six, or ten Action Steps are used to meet one objective. The goal may be listed at the top of several pages. The objective changes for each page as do the Action Steps for each objective. Thus, one, two, three, or however many objectives are needed to meet the goal are written, each on a new page. The goal remains the same but each new objective for that goal warrants a new page. (See Figure 4.1.)

The terminology and approaches used in writing objectives should be common to the organization and routinely used. Breaking down objectives can be useful for some projects, but for others it may be confusing. If the activities to be conducted need to be broken down into highly specified activities, action steps or sub-objectives will be useful. If the activity requires a great deal of detail, and it is necessary to ascertain who is responsible for the action, objectives can be broken down into two or three levels. However, some find the process of developing sub-objectives tedious and confusing. The approach that is most effective for the project at hand and the organization's expectations should be selected.

If sub-objectives are to be developed, they should be supportive of a general objective. Remember, general objectives are not goals but objectives. This means they are specific and measurable, and they have time limits set for completion, standards, conditions, or levels of performance that are expected to be met, and outcomes. Sub-objectives have the same criterion and parts that are used in general objectives, but are only used to meet the general objective. One general objective can have many sub-objectives.

How to Write Objectives. To be successful in writing objectives, one should keep several factors in mind.

1. Objectives must be performance, behavior, or action oriented.
2. Objectives must be precise in their language (do not use general or vague verbs).
3. Objectives must be measurable.
4. Objectives must be clear and state the level, condition, or standard of performance.
5. Objectives must be results oriented and have stated outcomes.
6. Objectives must have clarity in the descriptions of the content and performance.
7. Objectives must have a specific time for completion.[4,7,8,9]

In sub-objectives, persons responsible for accomplishing activities and for doing certain things and for outcomes could be named. Also, a list of verbs used to describe the action or performance is useful (see Table 4.1).

When taking on the actual task of developing and writing the objectives, many people find that the basic constructs as presented here are enough. That is, it is important to know that the written objectives must include: 1) the performance or action being stated, 2) a measurable factor, 3) a standard of performance or condition being stated, and 4) a time element.

Structured Approach to Writing Objectives

A second approach that is useful includes the presentation of a sentence structure with those elements that establish the sentence as an objective. The K I S S method should be kept in mind. The specificity

TABLE 4.1. *List of Verbs/Terms*

Less precise verbs	More precise verbs	
(Open to many interpretations—avoid using these terms)	(Open to few interpretations—try to select these or similar terms)	
	Intellectual level	*Feeling level*
know	discuss	challenges
realize	evaluate	defends
fully realize	identify	disputes
enjoy	list	joins
believe	diagram	judges
understand	compare and contrast	offers
really understand	translate	praises
feel responsible for	recall and state	questions
appreciate	integrate	shares
fully appreciate	illustrate	attempts
value	select	visits
comprehend	interpret	accepts
be aware of	differentiate	supports
tolerate	summarize	
be familiar with	classify	
desire	predict	
feel	apply	
have faith in	write	
grasp the significance of	recite	
acknowledge	solve	
know	construct	
be motivated	complete	
experience	prepare	
be informed of	make	
be involved in	run	
	draft	
	draw	
	contract	
	develop	
	open	
	define	
	describe	
	tabulate	
	answer	
	report	
	state	

and details of objectives can be overdone or become too complex, and this is to be avoided. Objectives are not policy statements; they are tools to help the planner become organized, effective, and efficient. Objectives force the planner to consider all activities, to think through all things that are important to the project, and to remember and account for everything that needs to be done. Objectives can be used in evaluation to assess work and progress of the planning effort, implementation efficiency and effectiveness, and the success of the project.

How to Use a Structured Approach

If the more general approach to actually writing objectives is not satisfactory or is hard to understand, a more structured approach is recommended. Using a preset structure to write out the objectives, all the planner has to do is plug in the desired words and the appropriate verbs and the objective is complete.

To	_____	_____	by	_____	at	_____.
	verb—	noun—		date—		cost or
	action	outcome		time		level or
						condition

Another approach also may be used.

By	_____	_____	_____	_____.
	time	verb—	noun—	condition
		action	outcome	or level

Appropriate connecting and descriptive words are to be added where needed. Simply write in the correct or desired words directly above the parts of the sentence that apply as shown in these structures.

The structure does not include the "who" part of the objective and fails to name who does it—the responsible person is not named. Thus, the structure should be preceded by a short statement that is a part of the objective. An example is: "By department head." If such a statement is written before a group of objectives, it saves time and effort since this part of the statement does not have to be repeated. (See Table 4.2.) With this approach to writing objectives, the planner simply fills in the blanks and other appropriate words and the objective is complete.

Table 4.2. The Health Promotion and Marketing Department Head will ...

by <u>April 15th,</u>	<u>run</u>	a <u>newspaper story</u> announcing the opening of the
time	verb	noun—
		outcome

new health promotion program for senior citizens <u>in 6 local newspapers</u>.

                                                                 level or standard

OR

<u>arrange</u> for several <u>TV spots</u>		by	<u>April 15th</u>, announcing the opening of the
verb	noun—		time
	outcome		

new outpatient clinic for senior citizens with <u>three different spots being</u>

                                                         level or condition

<u>shown on the 2 local TV stations</u>.

     level or condition

Verb Choice in Writing Objectives

When choosing verbs for objectives, the planner should select verbs that are specific and detailed, show action, and are not vague. One way to ensure that proper verbs are used, and vague and less effective verbs are not selected, is to use a list of verbs that show detail and action. Refer to the list of more precise verbs and less precise verbs in Table 4.1 for use in writing objectives.

A third method used to write objectives has been referred to as the *criteria approach.*[6] A checklist of elements is used to ascertain if all parts needed for an objective are included or are present in the objective. The criteria include:

1. Outcome
2. Action
3. Actor
4. Time
5. Proficiency
6. Measurement

PLANNING QUESTIONS

The planner needs to ask ...

☐ What results/outcomes are desired? (This question responds to the outcome, action, and actor criteria.)

☐ How will success be evaluated? (This question responds to the proficiency and measurement criteria.)

☐ When will the results occur? (This question responds to the time criterion.)[6]

Objective Writing Is Consistent Across the Board

It does not matter whether the planner uses the usual performance objectives approach or the objective and sub-objective approach. Writing regular objectives and writing sub-objectives use the same elements and the same approach.

PLANNING QUESTIONS

☐ What are the specific and detailed activities which need to be done and need to have objectives and/or sub-objectives written for them?

☐ Have several objectives been written for each goal?

☐ Do the goals and objectives clearly present what the project or program is planning to accomplish?

☐ Do the objectives clearly set forth the activities, time frame, responsible persons, outcomes, and level of performance needed for the objectives to be effective?

Common Errors in Goal and Objective Setting[7]

1. The planner fails to clarify common goals for the whole unit.
2. The planner sets goals and objectives too low and fails to maintain quality.

3. The planner does not use prior experience and results to find new answers.

4. The planner fails to develop and shape project objectives to fit the goals and mission of the organization.

5. The planner develops and exercises overkill through developing too many inappropriate or impossible-to-reach goals and objectives.

6. The planner fails to clearly assign responsibilities to the appropriate positions or people.

7. The planner allows two or more persons to believe they are responsible for the same tasks.

8. The planner focuses on how to do the job rather than on areas of responsibility.

9. The planner focuses on what is pleasing to him or her instead of focusing on accomplishing the objectives.

10. The planner fails to make clear guidelines and policies for the work and for accomplishing goals and objectives and then makes multiple subjective adjustments and changes resulting in confusion and disrupted goals and objectives.

11. The planner accepts other worker's goals uncritically without regard for the overall goal and mission statements.

12. The planner is reluctant to recognize higher administration's known desires and expectations.

13. The planner ignores obstacles that the program or project will face, including emergency or routine duties all of which consume a great deal of time.

14. The planner ignores the proposed new goals of subordinates or top administration and uses only those goals he or she deems suitable.

15. The planner does not think through or act on what he or she must do to help the project or program be successful.

16. The planner fails to introduce new ideas from outside of the organization or to permit workers to make suggestions.

17. The planner fails to set intermediate target dates or develop timelines by which to measure progress.

18. The planner fails to seize opportunities and instead clings rigidly to the plan, the objectives, and the goals without some flexibility.

19. The planner fails to allow previously agreed-on goals to be changed when they have proven unfeasible, irrelevant, or impossible to achieve.

20. The planner does not reinforce or recognize successes when objectives and goals are achieved.

21. The planner obsessively writes goals and objectives, does the planning process, but then fails to work the plan.

22. The planner forgets to include an evaluation process or fails to consider evaluation from the very beginning of the planning process.

Summary

Part I presents an overview of writing goals and objectives for the need assessment phase—the next step in the planning process. (See Planning and Program Development Model at the front of the book.) However, the main use of goals and objectives is to set forth the step-by-step activities and procedures necessary to develop the master plan for carrying out the overall project or program. These are presented in Part II.

Effective planning depends on clear and explicit written objectives that indicate exactly what the planner or administrator is to do. Objectives, when written in the context and structure as presented here, result in good planning objectives. Written objectives not only function well in assisting the planning process but also become invaluable in the evaluation of the program or project.

CHAPTER OBJECTIVES—PART II

The main purposes of Part II of this chapter are to:

1. Explain the role of goals and objectives in planning and program development.

2. Review goals and objectives in planning and program development.

3. Explain the different types and levels of objectives.

4. Understand how to write goals and objectives for planning and program development.

5. Present planning questions for goal and objective writing.

STEP 6

Writing Goals and Objectives

- Once a project is determined and approved by administration, goals and objectives are developed and written.

PART II—Writing Goals and Objectives for Planning and Program Development

Introduction

Program development goals and objectives describe what the administration hopes to be able to do on completion of the planning phase of a project, service, or program. As discussed in Part I, and in review, *goals* are general and usually lack a specific time element. *Objectives* are the specific activities and outcomes used to achieve goals. Objectives are measurable, expect results, and include a time element.

In Part I, the basics of writing goals and objectives were presented. The fundamental concepts and principles provided are applicable and useful in program development. The basics of objective writing remain the same even though used in different phases of program development. Therefore, the essential information of Part I applies here.

Objectives are basic to and essential for the planning process. Goals and objectives provide direction to both planner and administrator. Direction is shown through clearly stating what is aimed for, what activities need to be accomplished, what outcomes are expected, how the activities should be carried out, whether the activities are being accomplished, and if they are being completed on time. (See Chapter 9 on timelines.)

Properly stated planning objectives are not only useful but are essential to high-quality program development. Failure to properly write and prepare planning objectives leaves the planner and the administrator little direction in program development, implementation, and evaluation. However, properly stated objectives serve to communicate the activities and outcomes of the project to key administrative personnel. Objectives set forth the specific and detailed activities necessary to develop and implement a service, program, or project that is undergoing the planning process and the results anticipated.[11,12,13]

The Difference Between Goals and Objectives

Planning and program development goals and objectives are written in degrees or levels of specificity and detail. Goals are stated in general terms and can be very general ("to provide outpatient clinic services to the elderly"). Objectives can be very specific ("to provide, for elderly patients, outpatient podiatric clinics and services every Friday to at least 35 patients"). All planning activities have goals and specific objectives. It must be accepted by the planner and by administration that not all goals are stated in perfect form. However, in objective writing, the more specific the details of the activities, the clearer the planning process will be. Several goals and many objectives usually are presented in each phase of a plan.[11-14]

Importance and Value

Planning objectives, being very specific, are for the planning, implementation, and evaluation of new programs and services. They are to be administration oriented and are most helpful if they guide the implementation and management process.

Benefits

Several benefits are derived from developing planning objectives.[2,4,5]

1. Provided with clearly defined objectives to work toward, planners can design health promotion, health care, and social services to meet them.

2. Provided with clearly defined objectives, the administrator can evaluate the effectiveness of the service according to whether the goals and objectives are achieved.

3. Each program or service can be assessed based on the level of completeness and effectiveness with which each objective has been met.

4. Research has shown that administrators can be more effective in management activities if they use goals and objectives. Goals and objectives open lines of communication and expectations become clear. Clearcut direction is provided and guessing or mismanagement is minimized.

5. Provided with clearly specified objectives, program planners are able to set sequences of activities and outcomes expected and establish timelines for completion of each.

6. Knowing what activities are to be completed, it should be possible to eliminate unnecessary overlap or duplication of activities or events.

7. Administrators can better understand the program development and planning process when they can read the specific activities, via objectives, to be carried out.

8. Through clearly stated planning objectives, planners can explain and demonstrate to administration what is being accomplished and how the program development process works.

9. Provided with clearly defined objectives, planners and administrators can determine what level of development and implementation the project is at.[11,13,14]

Stating Planning Objectives and Outcomes

Part II of this chapter focuses on the program development and planning process surrounding objective development and use. As previously presented, objectives are to be precise and include the specific details necessary to effectively put plans into action. Recall that objectives are to be specific and measurable, have stated outcomes, and include a time element and a condition or standard that is to be met.

The success of the program will be contingent on the effectiveness of the objectives. If the objectives are well thought-out, are well developed, and contain enough detail about program activity and responsibility, program planning and implementation will go smoothly. Program management and evaluation also can experience greater success if there are well-developed and well-written objectives.

As a planning adage states: "Plan the work and work the plan." Writing objectives should not be just an exercise to be gone through. Planning and implementation of programs works only when the planner and the administrator put the plan into action. The plan must be taken seriously and be put to work. Objectives are the foundation of the planning process. They are only as important and as effective as the administrator makes them. If objectives are viewed as an exercise to be gone through and not earnestly used, the administration would be wiser to use the time, finances, and resources for some other administrative activity.

PLANNING QUESTIONS

In an effort to simplify the planning, objective writing, and development process consider the following:

☐ **Who** is responsible for performing the administrative activities? That is, who is to actually do the implementation and management of the program or part or phase of the program?

☐ **Performance** is the action part of the objective. This is where verbs are used that set forth precise and specific administrative performance. (See the list of action-oriented verbs in Table 4.1.)

☐ **Activities and results:** The results of the implementation and management of the program are to be measured and evaluated. Using goals with specific planning objectives sets forth what actual activities are to be done and how effectively they are being accomplished.

☐ **Conditions** set forth the location and conditions under which the planner or manager is to implement and manage the program—for example, at the clinic site, at the hospital, at the agency, at the senior citizens' center, or within the meals-on-wheels kitchen, within the contract negotiations.

☐ **Standards** set forth the expected level of competence or completion at which each activity must be implemented or managed. For example, levels are stated in percentages, dollars, numbers of activities, and so on.

Sample Objective

The 90-minute "Health Education for the Elderly" program will be conducted by the community health educator every Thursday at the hospital auditorium for one year with an attendance of 200 elderly persons. Each session will be on topics of keen interest to the elderly.

- Who = community health educator
- Performance = Health Education . . . program conducted
- Activities and results = health education for the elderly program . . . 200 elderly persons attending
- Conditions = at hospital auditorium
- Standards = 90 minutes, for one year, 200 attending each session, of keen interest to the elderly.

Be Precise in Writing Objectives

To be effective in planning and program development, it is a good idea to set up objectives with as much detail and information as necessary and to be as precise and specific as possible. The more precise one is in writing objectives, the more effective and efficient implementation and management will be. Thus, activities should be clearly thought out and clearly stated. Overly complex, overly long objectives using compound sentences are discouraged.

The use of more precise verbs (listed in Table 4.1) allows planning to be more exact and clear; evaluation becomes more precise as well. The use of verbs and adjectives that have general and vague meaning allows for the construction of objectives that contribute to ambiguity and confusion. It is much more advantageous to use the best terms to describe or define the performance and activities to occur. Precise terms strengthen the planning, implementation, evaluation, and management processes by providing better direction to both the planner and administrators. The manager will know what is expected.

The planner will better be able to provide detailed activities that both the planner and the manager will be able to understand, put into action, and better evaluate.[12,14,15]

When a pilot is getting an airplane ready to fly, he or she is required to use a checklist of everything that needs to be done and checked before the airplane is started. A second check is done using a checklist before the airplane is allowed to take off. Similar checklist activities and approaches are most useful for planners and managers. The use of the verb list is one checklist-related approach that is useful to the planner in writing objectives. Planning questions, as presented throughout this book, provide another form of checklist.[12,14,15]

Consistency and Congruency in the Planning Process

The planner has the responsibility for ensuring that the goals and objectives continue to address the priorities discovered in the need assessment process—Step 4 in Chapter 5. Additionally, the planner must continue to ensure that step-by-step planning and objective writing clearly set a pattern for implementation. This helps ensure that management will be effective and efficient.

The goals and objectives are to be congruent with the hopes, needs, and expectations of the culture and background of the target population. The planner has to be aware of and sensitive to the unique culture and traditions of the people who are to receive services. All goal and objective development should take any special needs and expectations of the group into account, whether they are Hispanic elderly, black older adults, Native Americans, or workers receiving health promotion at the worksite.

PLANNING QUESTIONS

☐ Has administration reviewed and approved the project to be planned and developed?

☐ Have goals been written for each part or phase of the program in order to ensure successful implementation and management of the program or service?

☐ Has an objective been written for each goal and for every specific activity and outcome needed for successful implementation and management of the program or service?

☐ Have all of the parts of an objective been included in each objective?

☐ Has evaluation been considered in the process of developing goals and objectives?

☐ Has a goal and objective been developed/written for all activities that need to be evaluated?

☐ Has an effort been made to ensure that each objective has the five elements: who is responsible, performance, activities and results, conditions, standards? Do they meet the criteria and approach presented in Part I?

☐ Are goals and objectives consistent and congruent with the previously determined priorities as discussed in Chapter 6?

☐ Do the goals and objectives provide clear direction toward the actual implementation and program management process?

References

1. Bloch, A. *Murphy's Law Book Three*. Los Angeles, CA: Price/Stern/Sloan, 1982.

2. Timmreck, T. C. *Dictionary of Health Services Management*, 2d ed. Owings Mills, MD: National Health Publishing, 1987.

3. Brickner, W. H. and Cope, D. M. *The Planning Process*. Cambridge, MA: Winthrop Publishers, 1977.

4. Mager, R. F. *Preparing Instructional Objectives*. Palo Alto, CA: Fearon Publishers, 1962.

5. MacStravic, R. E. S. *Marketing by Objectives for Hospitals*. Germantown, MD: Aspen Publishing, 1980.

6. Deegan, A. X. II. *Management by Objectives for Hospitals*. Germantown, MD: Aspen Publishing, 1977.

7. Nutt, P. C. *Planning Methods for Health and Related Organizations*. New York: Wiley, 1984.

8. Odiorne, G. S. *Management by Objectives, II*. New York: Fearon Pitman Publishing, 1979.

9. Dignan, M. B. and Carr, P. A. *Introduction to Program Planning: A Basic Text for Community Health Education*. Philadelphia: Lea & Febiger, 1981.

10. Numerof, R. E. *The Practice of Management for Health Care Professionals*. New York: AMACOM, 1982.

11. Kibler, R. J., et al. *Behavioral Objectives and Instruction*. Boston: Allyn and Bacon, 1970.

12. Odiorne, G. S. *Management by Objectives, II*. Belmont, CA: Fearon Pitman Publishing, 1979.

13. Brickner, W. H. and Cope, D. M. *The Planning Process*. Cambridge, MA: Winthrop Publishers, 1977.

14. Dignan, M. R. and Carr, P. A. *Introduction to Program Planning: A Basic Text for Community Health Education*. Philadelphia: Lea & Febiger, 1981.

15. Fodor, J. T. and Davis, Gus T. *Health Instruction: Theory and Application*. Philadelphia: Lea & Febiger, 1981.

Chapter 5

Need Assessments: Determining Programs and Services: Spanning the Gaps

BIONDI'S LAW

If your project doesn't work, look for the part you didn't think was important.

MURPHY'S LAW[1]

CHAPTER OBJECTIVES

The main purposes of this chapter are to:

1. Explain the role of need assessments.

2. Present planning questions for need assessment development.

3. Define need assessment.

4. Define and explain catchment area and target group.

5. Explain community resource assessment.

6. Explain the types and approaches to need assessments.

7. Provide key terms used in need assessments.

8. Review items used in needs assessment questionnaires and inventories.

9. Review and explain how to develop need assessment instruments.

10. Explain need assessment methodology.

11. Review the PRECEDE model of health promotion planning as a need assessment approach.

12. Review sampling in need assessment survey work.

13. Discuss the importance of training in the need assessments process.

14. Discuss the assessment of data and writing it up.

15. Discuss how to identify gaps in services as well as programmatic needs.

STEP 4

Need Assessments

- Identify the catchment area, the target group, the market—the group or population to be served.

- Complete a community assessment—assess and inventory existing community resources, services, and programs.

- Determine the type of need assessment method or approach—i.e., survey, focus groups, PRECEDE model, etc.

- Determine items to assess and items and issues to be covered by the need assessment.

- Develop a need assessment instrument.

- Develop need assessment methods and processes.

- Establish a training program for outreach workers/surveyors.

- Train outreach workers/surveyors to conduct the need assessment.

- Conduct the need assessment/survey.

- Analyze and assess the data and findings of the need assessment.

- Evaluate the importance of the results and write up findings.

- Determine results of the findings of the assessment of the community and its resources and programs.

- Identify gaps in services and programs, and identify need areas.

Overview of Need Assessments

Need assessments are basic to the planning process of any project or program being considered for development, yet little has been written on need assessments, their development or use. Many approaches to the assessment of the need for a project have been used. Need assessments range from informal approaches, using educated and informed observations, to formal, comprehensive research projects. However, the informal approaches are less reliable than a planned and scientifically developed research approach.

Educated observation used as a need assessment is often limited by the narrow views of the administrator, who sees the needed project only from his or her background and training, and from responsibilities of the position he or she occupies. Influenced by vested interests and hidden agendas, administrators may push for a favored project. For example, many health care administration professionals would guess (educated informant) that the main health care need of older adults is access to a clinic and medical insurance. Instead, formal research-oriented need assessments have shown, over and over, that transportation is the number one health care need of the elderly. (See Knowledge Leader section starting on page 93.)

Many administrators and planners often feel that the need assessment phase of planning is limited value and may forego it, believing they already know what the needs are and what is necessary to develop the project at hand. Limited time, personnel, and money are some of the reasons administrators give for foregoing the need assessment phase. Administrators have some justification for taking such a position; some enthusiastic planners/researchers have been known to turn what should be a simple need assessment into a major research project. These committed professionals use up scarce resources and time unnecessarily, when a simpler need assessment would have done the job.

The Role of Need Assessments

Need assessments are used to ascertain what resources, services, equipment, or other available items exist for use in the program being planned. Need assessments also are used to survey, assess, evaluate and do research on what services or programs exist and which services are missing. Missing parts of a project or program—gaps in services, desires, and interests of those who need to receive the services—are determined. Need assessments are that portion of the plan development process that involves assessment of program or project needs; it is done prior to setting priorities, aims, goals, and objectives.[2]

Two major issues arise when planning a need assessment. First, what is the target population, and second what is the catchment area of the project or service that is being planned? In program planning and development, a *target group* is defined as a community area or health promotion worksite population chosen as the recipient of a specially developed service: a service area, a community, or a special population that has been designated to receive services due to a demand for services or from an identified need associated with the population or locality.[2] Target groups can be selected by age, race, ethnicity, religion, accessibility, geographical location, worksite, and so on. A target group is a concentration of populations or clients that are the focus of a service. To be eligible to participate in or receive a service one might be required to be within the target population.[3]

A *catchment area* is a geographic area defined and served by a health promotion program or health care or social service on the basis of such factors as population distribution, roads and housing layouts, natural geographic boundaries, and accessibility to transportation. All residents of the area needing the services or the program usually are eligible for them, although eligibility may depend on additional criteria such as age or income. Residents of the catchment area may or may not be limited to services other than those obtainable from the program.

An appropriate geographical area is selected in which to conduct the need assessment—an area that will be served by the program and for which the program has responsibility.[2] The catchment area idea has been addressed in planning for community mental health services. In this context, Numerof suggests that the concept be used to define the size of the geographic area so it is manageable.[4]

Marketing research approaches, such as in-person and telephone surveys, interviews, focus groups, and community diagnosis, also may be of use to the program planner as need assessments approaches.

What is a *need assessment*? It is the process of identifying those programs or services in a geographical area or community that are in place and functioning well. It is also the process of identifying the lack of services and programs. Need assessments are used to identify gaps in services and needs, interests, and demands for a program or service. It is the act and process of determining the shortcomings and shortfalls of current services, activities, and programs. The need assessment activity is done so the planner can identify gaps in service and programs as well as problems in the current services and programs system. (See Figure 5.1.) Need assessments also can be used as a management tool, as part of the evaluation process, to make a program effective and efficient while improving the quality and quantity of services.

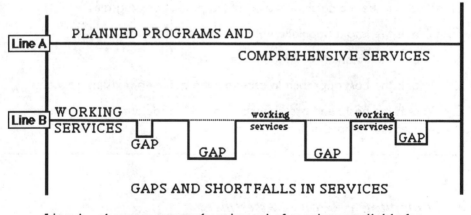

Line A shows a comprehensive set of services available for the target population.

Line B shows an existing set of services with some missing, leaving gaps in services as determined by the need assessments.

FIGURE 5.1. *Results of Need Assessments Identifying Gaps in Services*

Barriers to Services

Barriers to services must be considered when planning for a need assessment and the need assessment questionnaire. Anticipate and include any barriers that the planner or the program development team might foresee. Barriers to services and programs can be broadly addressed in terms of availability, accessibility, cost, efficiency, quality, and continuity of programming. Barriers in each of these six areas can be listed and spelled out by the program development team in a brainstorming session or a Delphi process.

For the need assessment questionnaire and process to be effective, the planner has to have a good understanding of and a comprehensive familiarity with the population, geographical area, and existing services and programs. In the actual need assessment, the identification of needs and the need assessment process should be limited to the target population and the changes that are occurring in the select and targeted group.

PLANNING QUESTIONS

☐ Can the population and geographical area be identified?

☐ What is to be the catchment area of the project or program?

☐ What is the target population of the project or program?

☐ What is the "market" or group to be served?

☐ What is the best approach to ascertain the quality of existing services?

☐ What is the best need assessments approach to determine the gaps in services and programming?

Community Resource Assessment

When making preparations to do an assessment of community resources, the planner should have plans to develop a report or a booklet on completion of the assessment. The amount, extent, and type of community resource assessment depends on the scope of the project or service being planned. Area agencies on aging, public health departments, social service departments within hospitals, and so on may develop a complete booklet or resource binder of all related agencies in the county, region, city, or catchment area. If the project is specialized, such as the development of an Alzheimer's center or an outpatient clinic for senior citizens, only those resources, supportive services and activities, and agencies that directly or indirectly relate to the program or project should be assessed and included in the report.

Improper need assessment approaches can limit objective findings. Need assessments, especially in populations with true needs, can create expectations and high hopes. In the process of doing surveys—asking people questions and doing interviews—hopes rise about the needed programs becoming actual services, which are then anticipated. If people are asked if they want programs developed, they soon determine from the questions and need assessment experience what it is all about and get high hopes (and even false hopes) about programs that could be coming their way.

In part, health promotion program development relies on health status indicators of the target population. Those risk factors contributing to disease, conditions, injury, disability, and death, as identified by public health statistics and human services data, often are used in the need assessments process. Examples of such data are shown in the figures in Chapter 1.

Need Assessment Approaches

Many different approaches to need assessments have been utilized. Seven methods are more commonly used than others. Many types of need assessments are used, and new and different approaches are developed as a need arises or a particular discipline finds a special interest in a more definitive approach, such as the PRECEDE model used for health promotion planning. Several methods used most often are presented here in the order of least preferred to most preferred.

Knowledgeable Leader/Key Informant Approach

The experience and knowledge of key community leaders, informed individuals, and professional persons who are well aware of and in touch with the needs of the target population of concern are viewed as valuable. From the knowledgeable leader, insights and information are gathered on the needs of the target population and the community. It is assumed that since they hold key positions in the community, these persons are most likely to be familiar with the population being assessed and can offer good insights into the needs, gaps in services, and resources available. The limitations of this approach to need assessments are quite obvious. Leaders with hopes of programs coming their way or a vested interest in certain services that could be developed may slant their observations or be less than objective in their assessments and recommendations.

The methodology used in Knowledgeable Leader/Key Informant usually involves putting a roster of knowledgeable leaders and key informants together. Three approaches can be used with this method:

1. A short questionnaire could be developed and used with several knowledgeable leaders and key informants to standardize what could be a lot of personal opinion. The form should leave room to write in anecdotal observations. The questionnaire is filled out in an interview type situation. Analysis of results could be done using the Delphi method.

2. Self-completed questionnaires could be filled out by several knowledgeable leaders and key informants using a standardized form.

3. Semi-structured interviews could be done in person or over the phone.

The concern of this subjective approach is for maintaining accuracy of information, standardizing the question-asking process, minimizing vested interest, and downplaying subjective opinion. Thus, the more structured the approach, questions, and questionnaire, the more objective the information will be. The same questions are used with all Knowledgeable Leaders/Key Informants. If all questions are written out and used in a uniform manner, plus having the responses recorded in a uniform manner, tabulation and analysis of the data will be easier, accuracy will increase, and the process will be more objective—the data-gathering process will be more valid and reliable.

Community Forum

Public meetings are planned, announced, and widely advertised to the target population in the community. The community meetings are held with the target population and related and interested professionals.

Key leaders are invited from key organizations and agencies, aiming for a good representation. For the public meeting to be successful, extensive public education and advertising must be conducted. Transportation, food or refreshments, and other incentives could be provided in order to get an adequate turnout of members from the target group at the public meeting.

Once the public meeting is underway, several approaches could be used: 1) Key questions to be answered could be presented to the audience; responses and comments can be recorded and analyzed later. 2) The brainstorming approach could be effective in such a meeting. 3) Questionnaires could be given to all of those attending and retrieved at the end of the meeting. Results of the brainstorming session could use a modified Delphi method approach. A series of small neighborhood-based meetings could be held using some or all of the above-mentioned approaches.

Rates Under Treatment Approach

The Rates Under Treatment (RUT) approach is based on the use of services. That is, those persons who use the service or program become the source of expertise on the needs, shortcomings, and gaps in service of the program. It is believed that the recipients of the service are representative of others needing the service not yet using it. Medical records, or organizational records, also have been used as sources of data and information to establish needs. Demographic information is utilized to develop the database and establish needs. Basic and commonly gathered demographic and information data, which is routinely entered in medical and personnel records, can be lifted from the organization's records. The data usually includes:

- Age
- Race
- Income
- Sex
- Marital status
- Types of service used
- Amount of services consumed
- Presenting problems and diagnosis if medically related and useful
- Frequency of visits or use

- Results of use
- Satisfaction with service
- Length of stay if at a medical-related facility

Patterns of use, resources used, geographical origin, and related information can come from records kept by many organizations. It is harder to identify gaps in services with the RUT approach because it lacks a way of asking what is missing, what services or programs are needed, what are the shortcomings, or what is desired by the participant or consumer of the service.

Social and Health Status Indicators Approach

The need for programs or services can be established from health, social, and demographic indicators. In the RUT method, as discussed above, the information comes from local organizations' records. The records used to ascertain social indicators are those of the state and local public health departments, department of vital statistics, insurance companies, census records, and any other public agency that keeps useful records on the community and/or the target population. Most data comes from government-generated reports instead of from the individual organization. Epidemiological information sources that produce health status and social indicators are useful and include information in these forms:

- Dot maps
- Geographical and topographical factors
- Demographic data
- Sociological data
- Vital statistics
- Acute disease incidence and prevalence rates
- Chronic disease, and lifestyle and behaviorally caused incidence and prevalence rates
- Risk factor incidence and occurrence
- Accessibility to and use of health services
- Health promotion, prevention, and control practices or lack of them

All these pieces of epidemiological information must be linked to various indicators and measures of delivery of health and social services:

- Accessibility
- Acceptability
- Quality
- Availability
- Cost
- Continuity of services
- Comprehensiveness of services
- Capacity

Generalized assumptions about needs for services are ascertained by the epidemiological and demographic data. Other data about levels of providers of services—i.e., physicians per 1000 population, physician visits, levels of knowledge, health practices, and so on—can be obtained from professional associations and state and federal agencies. The planner has the responsibility for accurately extrapolating this data to fit and meet local needs and gaps in services. The shortcoming of this approach is that data is generalized from a large population, and then it is expected to fit local needs. Specific needs and specialized programs are not considered in this method and approach. Additionally, this approach falls short of actually identifying needs and gaps in services specific to the target population in the community at hand.

Service Population Approach

The Service Population approach focuses on a specific target population and uses techniques similar to marketing techniques. Barriers to services, needs, and problems are identified. The Knowledgeable Leader/ Key Informant approach could be incorporated into this approach as could the survey approach.

Three methods are used in the Service Population approach to gather data; the approach is aimed at the consumers of the services.

Standardized questions or questionnaires are developed. The three methods are:

1. Person-to-person interviews
2. Mailed questionnaires
3. Telephone interviews

   This approach allows for insights into actual and real needs of the clientele. The added benefit of using this approach is that problems and barriers to service are identified. An advantage is that the Service Population approach identifies the needs and needed changes of the target population. This also can be a limitation as it focuses only on those included in the assessment process. The planner should try to anticipate what program needs, gaps in services, and barriers may be encountered in the development of the project. The planner should develop questions to address anticipated needs, gaps in services, and barriers to services.

Focus Groups

Focus groups have been used most often in marketing research. Ten to 12 average persons—consumers or potential consumers of a service—are asked to participate in a session. Three to 15 different focus groups are held with new participants each time. Five or six well-thought out and well-developed questions are used for every session. Each session is videotaped. The planner, when finished with all focus groups, reviews the tapes and makes a grid of comments and develops a database from them. Comments, trends, problems, and concerns that keep surfacing are noted and indicated in the grid, which becomes the database. A good facilitator has to conduct the focus groups and is not to lead the group's comments or thinking. The participants should feel free to make any comment they wish. The facilitator is not to let one outspoken person control the time and comments, while drawing comments out of the more quiet persons.

Community Diagnosis Approach

Health promotion and health education activities have benefited most from this need assessments approach. The PRECEDE-PROCEED Model was developed for use in health promotion and health education planning but could be adapted for human and social services. *PRECEDE* stands for *p*redisposing, *r*einforcing, and *e*nabling *c*onstructs in *e*ducational, *d*iagnosis, and *e*valuation activities. *PROCEED* stands for *p*olicy, *r*egulatory, *o*rganizational, *e*ducational, and *e*nvironmental *d*evelopment use to support the PRECEDE need assessment activities with resource mobilization, implementation, and evaluation.

PRECEDE accounts for the multiple factors that affect health status and assist the planner in focusing on those factors identified by this framework for intervention through programs and services. Criteria for evaluation can be developed from the activities of the PRECEDE model. Deductive thinking is required when using the PRECEDE model. To use the model, one works backward from phase one. The PRECEDE model is shown in Figure 5.2. The factors and processes of the PRECEDE model are presented in summary form in a framework structure in the figure.[5]

Survey Approach

The survey approach was reserved for presentation last because it is the most widely used. Survey research can be a complex and sophisticated design or it can be as simple as a one-page questionnaire addressing the needs of the project and the target population.

Prior to using surveys in a need assessment, several basic survey research issues need to be considered. First, one has to have a good questionnaire (see Figure 5.3). Question and questionnaire development requires spending a good deal of time to be sure that a useful and effective questionnaire is developed. Questions should be simple and straightforward. They should be asked in a manner that will ascertain need. Wording of the questions is most important and each should be edited and reviewed to ensure that each is prepared well and actually asks what it is supposed to. Avoid writing double negatives into questions. (Examples from an actual need assessment questionnaire: "He has no car, yes or no?" "There is no bus near by, yes or no?") Good questions ask what you want to know—what you want to find out—in a direct and simplified manner.

Keep the questions and the questionnaires short and to the point.

Sampling the Population

A good sampling approach is essential. A survey has to have validity and should use recognized methodologies. The number of persons participating in the survey has to be substantial enough to produce

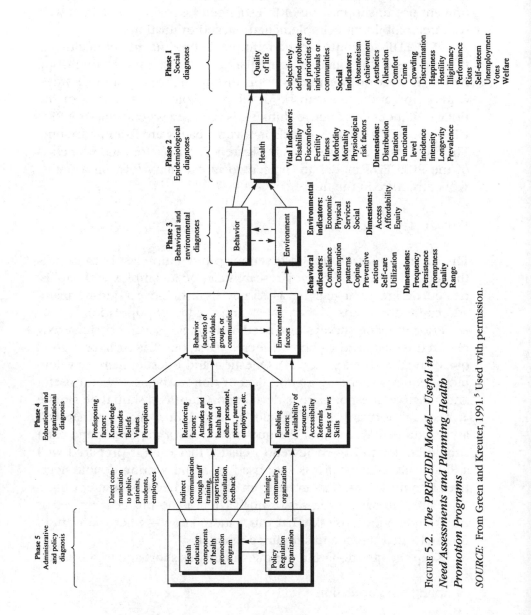

FIGURE 5.2. *The PRECEDE Model—Useful in Need Assessments and Planning Health Promotion Programs*

SOURCE: From Green and Kreuter, 1991.[5] Used with permission.

SAMPLE NEED ASSESSMENT SURVEY

Number ____

☐ 1. Name_____

☐ 2. Address_____

☐ 3. Zip code _____

☐ 4. Age_____

☐ 5. Race ☐Cau ☐Black ☐Hispanic ☐Asian ☐Native American ☐Other

☐ 6. Marital status _____

☐ 7. Sex_____

Transportation

☐ 8. Do you drive? ☐yes ☐no

☐ 9. Type of tranportation used most often? _____

☐ 10. Bus near by? ☐yes ☐no

☐ 11. Do you have enough money for the fare? ☐yes ☐no

☐ 12. Have limited ability to obtain transportation? ☐yes ☐no

Finance

☐ 13. Do you currently work for a salary? ☐yes ☐no

☐ 14. Do you work? ☐part-time ☐full-time

☐ 15. What range does your income fall within?

☐ $5,000 or less

☐ $5,000 to $10,000

☐ $10,000 to 20,000

☐ $20,000 to 30,000

☐ $30,000 to 40,000

☐ $40,000 to 50,000

☐ $50,000 to 60,000

☐ $60,000 to 75,000

☐ $75,000 or more   **page 1**

FIGURE 5.3. *Sample of the First Page of a Need Assessment Form*

results that are valid and reliable and give a true and accurate representation of the needs of the target population. Obtain as large a sample size as is feasible; the more participants in the survey the better. In other words, the larger the sample size the better.

Retrieving the Questionnaires

A major problem in survey research is retrieving the questionnaires once they are completed; therefore, a system for retrieving them needs to be established. Data-gathering systems can be coordinated with questionnaire retrieval; some approaches lend themselves to retrieval and solve sample size and questionnaire retrieval matters—for example, interviews and home visits. There needs to be a set system of follow-up for questionnaire retrieval, either by personally collecting them, having a trusted colleague at a workplace assist, or having a mail-in system with a follow-up process established.

Five Approaches to Data Gathering

Five approaches to gathering need assessment data are presented here. The approach should keep imposition on the interviewer to a minimum, yet not shortchange the interview or the data-retrieving process. The process should be done in a manner that ensures that the data is obtained and the questionnaires can be easily retrieved or sent in. Two of the greatest problems in survey research are: 1) to obtain the participation of the subjects/respondents, and 2) to retrieve the data (questionnaires).

1. *Person-to-person interviews* using the survey form/questionnaire. Interview at the potential recipients' homes, worksites, a senior citizen center, or in a shopping mall.

2. *Drop off the questionnaire* and return to retrieve it at a set time and date. This can be less of a burden to the person being interviewed because it allows them to fill it out at their own pace and at their convenience. The interviewee needs to be clearly informed of the time of retrieval and asked to have the questionnaire ready and waiting. This would work best in housing projects, senior high-rise apartments, and health promotion worksites.

3. *Mailed questionnaires*—the survey form is mailed to a predetermined list of individuals. Mailing lists are gathered to represent the target population, and/or potential recipients of the program. For example, mailing lists could be obtained from a senior high-rise apartment complex, a housing project for the elderly, a senior citizen's center, the county's Office on Aging, AARP chapters, and so on.

4. *Telephone interviews*—a survey form is used for telephone interviews to ensure accuracy and consistency in the gathering of data. Names and phone numbers could be obtained from sources similar to those mentioned under mailed questionnaires.

5. *Newsletter or magazine surveys*—a short or abbreviated survey form can be inserted in a newsletter or regional magazine with a self-stamped mailing arrangement included. Some sort of a folded survey form with the address and mailing stamp on the outside so the respondent can easily remove it, complete, fold, and mail usually works well.

Sample Selection

Sample selection is important. Sampling is a fundamental research skill and activity and requires the planner to take into account the kind of need assessment one wishes to use and the kinds of findings anticipated. The typical empirical research approaches to sampling are useful in need assessments. However, the more complex sampling approaches may not be necessary or appropriate for a need assessment. With regard to sampling approach, the size of the sample must be large enough to be able to show a true need and be representative of the population of recipients of the planned service or program. The reason for sampling is to get responses that show a true picture of need and to obtain reliable data that can be analyzed. Most of all the reason to use sampling is to cut cost and effort and yet be able to predict the need, as opposed to surveying an entire population.

Sample Size

A rough rule about sample size is: Use as large a sample size as possible or that is realistic. Statistical curves show that the smaller the sample size, the larger the error in predictability. The larger the sample, the smaller the error in predictability. Budget and the predictability—level of confidence—also determine sample size. Ordinarily, a few hundred questionnaires would be a good goal to aim for.[6,7]

Some of the sampling approaches that may be useful for need assessments research include:

Sample of convenience—This sampling approach works as long as the sample is large and includes possible recipients of the service. Generalizations are drawn from the findings and applied to the larger population. Even though this is one of the most commonly used approaches, it is one that lends itself to much bias and often is criticized by behavioral science researchers.[6,7,8]

Random sample of potential recipients. This approach is valid as long as the sample is quite large and the selection process uses a true random approach, i.e., cutting up a list of names and picking a set percentage out of a large container; choosing every fifth person from a computer printout of all the senior citizens in the target group or catchment area; and so on.

Random has two dimensions. One is random selection and the other is random assignment. *Random assignment* is assigning people to groups so that each person has an equal chance of being in the group to fill out the survey form. *Random selection* is the selection of individuals who will participate as subjects from the target population. Random selection is used in need assessments more often than random assignment.

Another issue is generalizing to populations or generalizing across populations. The tendency in need assessments is to generalize *to populations.* The program planner needs to be aware that when generalizing there is a risk of not meeting the needs of subgroups within the target populations. This occurs even when using random samples. To generalize *across populations* the planner may or may not wish to take the subpopulation's special interests into account. An example would be assessing food interests of older adults in a delivered meals program. A random sample shows that certain generic foods are preferred. The population is further studied and it is found that a major subgroup of Hispanics lives in the catchment area. However, they were not well represented in the sampling process, and they prefer more traditional Mexican food and may not receive it.[6,7,8]

Self-selection/Volunteer participation—In this sampling approach, a survey would be given to senior citizens who are willing to fill out the form at a senior center, somewhat of a sample of convenience. As a general rule this sampling approach has more bias in it than other forms. Research has shown that certain types of people participate more than others in filling out research forms. Characteristics of the type of people who are willing to fill out a survey form usually are: more educated, higher occupational status, great need for approval, high IQ, and low in authoritarianism.[6,8]

Blanket survey—This approach tries to interview all possible recipients of a service or program. A blanket survey is almost impossible to accomplish. Some need assessment programs sponsored by the federal government in the past have completed need assessments of 75 percent to 80 percent of all elderly in a county.[9,10] This approach supports the notion that the larger the sample size, the smaller the error in predicting need. This is very costly, and therefore is not used that often.

Stratified sample—The approach involves dividing the target population into two or more segments and sampling a different proportion of each. This process is most often based on some demographic characteristic or other variable in order to divide the population into a strata or segment. Random sampling is used.[6,8]

Cluster sample—This approach to sample selection is used if the target population is dispersed or is in separate places or spread over a large geographic area. It lends itself better to mail surveys and is less practical for interview or telephone approaches. If travel time and costs are high for interviews, cluster sampling will be economical. Random sampling is used. A large sample size needs to be maintained; if not, do not use cluster samples.[6,8]

Quota sample—When a stratified sample would be possible, this approach may be useful. If the interview approach is used, a quota sample may be a good method. Random sampling should be used. Interviewers are assigned a quota of a given number of interviews from each segment or cluster.[5]

Sample bias is important to consider and avoid. Many types of bias are possible. *Visibility bias*—only those who are identifiable or are at hand are included and those who are not easily identifiable are excluded. *Order bias*—people are chosen by alphabetical order, numerical order, or other means of sequential ordering. The tendency is to use people at the beginning too often and the end people (names) are rarely included. *Accessibility bias* occurs most often when field workers are allowed to pick the sample. They tend to pick those persons who are most easily reached. *Cluster bias* happens when the clusters are specified too close together because those who live near each other may interact and share information. *Affinity bias* is when people interview those to whom they tend to be drawn.[5,6,7] (See Table 5.1.)

TABLE 5.1. *Sample Selection Issues to Consider*

1. Be sure to sample the more visible and the more obscure portions of the target population equally.
2. Sampling should be done in a systematic order so as not to sample some groups or areas more than others.
3. Controls and incentives must be used to ensure that all respondents have an equal chance to be selected.
4. If the target population is clustered, there must be equal sampling within the clusters as well as between them.
5. If surveyors can pick their own sample and respondents, a way to control for any affinity to be drawn to like personnel must be in place.
6. If respondents are to self-select, they should be excluded from interaction with others being surveyed.
7. Bias must be reduced and controlled. Are some respondents more likely to respond than others or respond in a certain way? How can this be controlled?

SOURCE: Adapted from Alreck and Settle, *The Survey Research Handbook.*[6]

Internal and External Need Assessment

Strengths, Weaknesses, Opportunities, and Threats (SWOT)

Referred to as a SWOT analysis, this technique looks at the internal factors (strengths, weaknesses) and external factors (opportunities and threats). Actually used as a part of strategic planning, this can be useful to determine needs within an organization.

Method and Process

A group of six to 10 individuals are gathered in a room with a chalk board, white board, or large paper pad, and the facilitator conducts a brainstorming session. Everyone's comments are valid and all comments are to be written down on the board as they are stated. The facilitator uses this process for all four factors: strengths, weaknesses, opportunities, and threats. Then a person, often the facilitator, copies all of the responses from the board and synthesizes the words down into a list combining similar items. Then the list is taken to a management team meeting and a discussion is conducted on which items are needs that need to be filled. The most valuable items are those that fall under weaknesses and threats, as these are the areas that demonstrate needs. SWOT analyses are conducted at various levels within the organization from the board of directors down to the executive management team, from mid-level managers down to line employees. Also, persons from the community or patients can be included in SWOT analyses.

Strengths are used to determine internal functioning of the health services organization. What is considered under strengths includes issues under the control of the management team of the organization: anything in the organization or any service that may lead to an advantage over competitors; any internal service that can be strengthened and enhanced in order to lead to a benefit to the clients or patients of an organization.

Weaknesses are also used to determine internal functioning of the health services organization. Those weakness issues under the control of the management team are considered and brainstormed. Any internal issue or function or lack of service that may cause a disadvantage relative to competitors must be considered and developed.

To determine external functioning opportunities, issues and external factors are brainstormed on the board. The things that are considered include anything in the external environment that may assist the organization in reaching its goal. Concern is focused on major forces that can affect the health services industry. This is a chance to review services that are working well and see what can be done to enhance them, or reach a new market or catchment area.

Threats, when brainstormed on to the board, can help identify the potential gaps in services and insights can be gained into which new services to develop. The group brainstorms on the board the major unfavorable situation in the external environment. The group helps to identify those issues or factors which may prevent the health services organization from reaching the citizens. It also allows for the opportunity to review what the competitors are doing and what their potential is to develop new competitive services.

Training—An Important Part of the Need Assessments Process

Little has been written about the training aspect of the need assessments process. However, anyone experienced in survey research would testify to the importance of good training of interviewers, of those who conduct the need assessment, and of those professionals involved in filling out the questionnaire. The training should include:

- The goals and objectives of the research.
- The philosophical issues and foundational ideas behind the research.
- What the need assessment findings are to be used for.
- How questions are to be presented.
- Informal observations to be identified and recorded.
- How to conduct the interview.
- Logistic and administrative issues and concerns.
- Timelines and administrative constraints.
- Sampling matters and issues.
- Valid, reliable, and honest data-collection processes.
- Interview practice and role-playing.

Each project and need assessment attempt presents unique and separate issues, concerns, and specialized training needs. Training should be adapted for each project. It is most efficient to gather all surveyors together at one time for training. A proper educational setting, such as a classroom environment, should be used for such training. One key part of the training process is the interview practice and role-playing.

The surveyor should become acquainted with the questionnaire and issues related to and behind the research/need assessment. The role-play process is essential in acquainting the surveyor with the questionnaire and any potential problems or questions that may arise. The role-playing process is useful to solve problems or answer questions that would be hard to do once in the field.

PLANNING QUESTION

☐ Has training for need assessments research activities been considered and planned for?

Assessment of Data and Presentation of Findings

Even though the need assessment process is a form of survey research, evaluating the data in some cases does not need be as complex as formal scientific research, which relies heavily on inferential statistics for analysis of the data. Need assessment analysis does not always have such a requirement; they are meant to ascertain need. Probability and levels of chance are not as important to need assessments as they are to empirical and formal scientific research.

The need assessment process is not so much an academic exercise as it is a management and planning tool used for identifying areas of need. Thus, the focus is not on levels of significance as found in statistic texts. The findings are supposed to concentrate on individual needs. Percentages and statistics are not the issue; the amount of risk and jeopardy faced by individuals due to the lack of services, or inability to access health and social services, is.

Once the data is analyzed, it has to be laid out in a manner that can be easily understood and meaning can be put to it. Grids, tables, and charts are basic techniques.

Descriptive Statistics in Presenting the Findings

The following four classifications of observations of data are basic to descriptive statistics.

1. *Nominal Scale*—These are categories of data that have no order in a number (numerical) sense. Examples of nominal data are: sex, religion, ethnic origin, age, and so on. If these items are numbered, the numbers are only labels unless converted into some sort of data set.

2. *Ordinal Scale*—This classification provides order among the categories. The traditional Likert scale or range-type scale is the most common use of the ordinal scale. Table 5.2 is an example of the typical 5-point scales. The items or issues of measurement using the ordinal scale are determined by the need of the study. The terms (describing satisfaction) used in the example are not necessarily what may need to be measured in a need assessment situation. The example shown is to demonstrate the typical Likert scale often used when writing questions for a questionnaire.

TABLE 5.2. *Five-point Likert Scale Demonstrating the Use of the Ordinal Scale*

Question:		How satisfied are you with the quality of the meals delivered in the Meals-on-Wheels program?		
1	2	3	4	5
highly dissatisfied	dissatisfied	average	satisfied	highly satisfied

3. *Interval Scale*—This scale is a numerical scale and has intervals between the items, categories, or units of measurement. The interval scale also has *no zero point*. IQ measurement as shown on the bell curve normal distribution is an example of this scale because it has no zero point; 100 is the midpoint on the bell curve and represents normal or average IQ.

4. *Ratio Scale*—This is the same as the interval scale but *has a zero point*; it relies on an equal distance between points on the scale: 50 is half the amount of 100, 15 is half the amount of 30, and so on.

PLANNING QUESTIONS

☐ As a planner, do you think the best need assessments approach and questionnaire have been considered?

☐ Has the type of data the different types of scales produce been considered and reviewed?

☐ Has the data scale that will produce the proper data and information needed or necessary to plan the service or program been selected?

Using Tables to Present Data

Initially tables are the best way to present data. Tables are called "tabular presentations of data." The planner should construct tables that show the frequency of scores. Scores, numbers, or the frequency of numbers are presented in table form and are called "frequency tables" or "frequency distribution tables." Examples of frequency tables are shown in Tables 5.3 and 5.4.

TABLE 5.3. *Frequency Table Showing Interval/Ratio Scale*

Age Grouping of Elderly Participants—Frequency Distribution

Category:Age Groups	Frequency
55 to 60	45
61 to 65	56
66 to 70	65
71 to 75	34
76 to 80	32
81 plus	22

Graphic Presentation of Data

Six basic types of graphic presentations are commonly used in making a pictorial presentation of the data of the need assessment. The six types of graphic presentations which are commonly produced by computer programs are: area, bar, column, line, pie chart, and scattergram. Examples of these are shown in Figures 5.4 to 5.9. These graphs and charts are computer generated.

Depending on the computer software program, charts and graphs can come in a variety of other shapes and arrangements. Traditional descriptive statistics usually are presented in forms somewhat like these computer-generated charts. Three additional representations of charts or graphs are shown in Figures 5.10 to 5.12. These charts are representative of the four types of scales mentioned above. Bar charts also can be presented in a vertical fashion (called columns in computer-generated charts).

TABLE 5.4. *Frequency Table Showing the Ordinal Scale*

Satisfaction with Delivered Meals Program—Frequency Distribution

Category	Frequency
Very dissatisfied	5
Dissatisfied	8
Average	55
Satisfied	79
Very satisfied	49

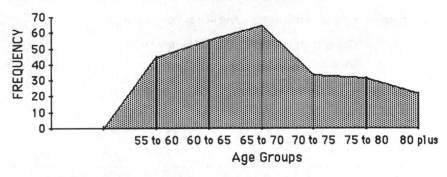

FIGURE 5.4. *Area Graph*

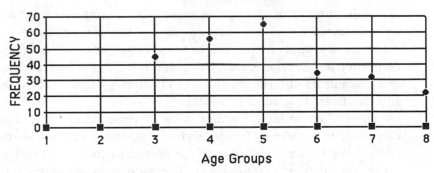

FIGURE 5.5. *Scattergram Graph*

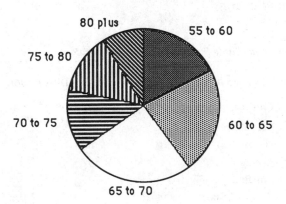

FIGURE 5.6. *Pie Chart*

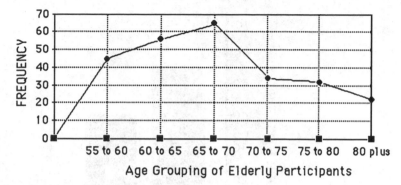

FIGURE 5.7. *Line Graph*

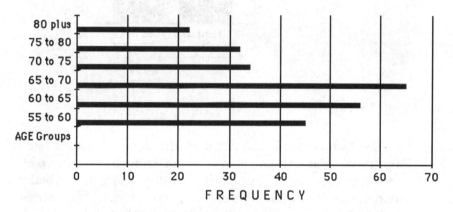

FIGURE 5.8. *Bar Graph (one approach, computer generated)*

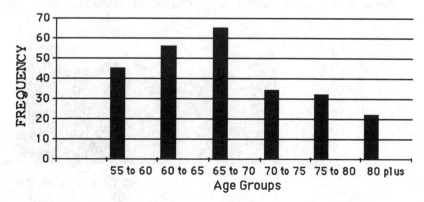

FIGURE 5.9. *Column Graph*

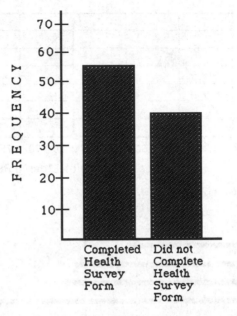

FIGURE 5.10. *Example of Bar Graph for Nominal Data*

Two factors are fundamental to the construction of bar charts. First, the bar width should always be the same for each bar. If each bar is not the same width, the different widths will give a visual presentation of the data being different—i.e., wider bars would mean larger numbers, narrower bars would give the idea of smaller in size or less in numbers. The height of the bars should be the only variable to present visual differences in the data. (See Figure 5.10.) Second, the space between the bars should be the same for each bar, be consistently

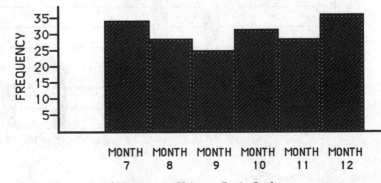

FIGURE 5.11. *Example of Histogram Using a Ratio Scale*

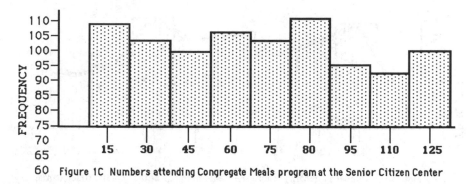

Figure 1C Numbers attending Congregate Meals program at the Senior Citizen Center

FIGURE 5.12. *Example of Histogram Using an Interval Scale*

spaced, be close enough to get a good visual comparison, and not be spaced wide distances apart.

Interval and ratio scales data are presented in a manner that resembles bar graphs but is different due to the data that is used. The presentation of interval and ratio scales is through a histogram. The bottom line (X axis or abscissa) uses the numbers of the data rather than labels. The frequency is presented on the Y axis. Figure 5.11 presents an example of the interval scale data used in a histogram, and Figure 5.12 shows ratio scales in a histogram.

The histogram shown in Figure 5.11 is a bar graph presentation of interval scale data. It is important that each interval between the numbers be equal. If a 1/2-inch wide bar (interval) is used for one, all intervals and bars must be 1/2-inch wide along the entire chart. The exact same data also can be presented in a line graph type chart, which is called a "frequency polygon." The frequency polygon presents exactly the same information as the histogram but is done differently pictorially, using a line instead of bars. Figure 5.13 is a frequency polygon overlaid on the histogram showing both are the same numerically and differ only pictorially. In addition, the frequency polygon using the same data as the histogram (interval scale) is shown in Figure 5.14.

Descriptive Statistics

At the minimum, the planner should present the basic findings of the need assessments in basic descriptive statistics form in a *need assessment report*. Tables for the descriptive statistics should also be shown. The main descriptive statistics should include central tendency:

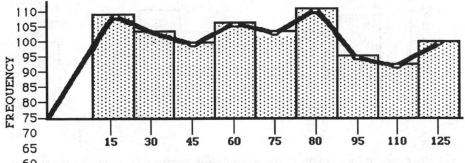

Figure 1C Numbers attending Congregate Meals program at the Senior Citizen Center

FIGURE 5.13. *Example of Frequency Polygon (line graph) Overlaid on a Histogram to Show Commonality of Both Type Charts Using Interval Scale Data*

mode, median, and mean. *Mode* is the most often occurring number; *median* is the middle number, which divides the distribution of numbers exactly in half; and *mean* is the arithmetic average. Other useful descriptive statistics include range, variance, and standard deviation.

Percentages are useful descriptive statistics to present if done correctly. Percentage can provide a clear picture of data or can mislead if presented incorrectly. Percentages always should be compared to the total number from which they come. For example, to show how many participated in a flu immunization program, the planner could say 88 percent of the participants were immunized. This percentage is meaningless. Is the data 88 percent of 10 or 88 percent of 1200 citizens?

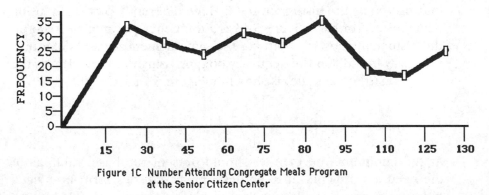

Figure 1C Number Attending Congregate Meals Program
at the Senior Citizen Center

FIGURE 5.14. *Example of Frequency Polygon (line graph) Using Interval Scale Data*

Therefore, when showing percents, always present the total number of the participants or the "*N*."

N stands for number of subjects. It is used in statistics to show the total number in the study population or any subgroup that is being compared statistically. The best way to show percentages is to state the *N* along with the percent—for example, "670 out of 750 or 89.3 percent of the participants in an elderly housing project request a health screening program."

Rates—comparing occurrences to groups of 100 or 1000 or 10,000—are commonly used descriptive statistics and epidemiology and may serve the planner well in presenting some portions of the data. Ratios are also a common form of descriptive statistics and may be of value to the planner under the appropriate circumstances. Percentages and rates are commonly used in public health planning reports. These can serve the program development process well if used appropriately with the type of data concerns, needs, or issues effectively demonstrated by this form of descriptive statistic.

PLANNING QUESTIONS

☐ What type of need assessment report do you need to prepare?

☐ Which data would best demonstrate the findings and needs to be presented in the need assessment report?

☐ What type of tables would best present the appropriate data showing the needs and findings?

☐ What type of graphs and charts would best show the data and present the needs found by the need assessment?

☐ Which graphs and charts would best demonstrate gaps in services and programs?

☐ Which data should be shown in descriptive statistics form?

☐ Would inferential statistics enhance the report and better demonstrate need?

☐ Is a formal presentation of the need assessment findings required? If so, which kind of graphic presentations would show the need, gaps, and concerns found by the need assessment?

References

1. Bloch, A. *Murphy's Law Book Three*. Los Angeles: Price/Stern/Sloan, 1982.
2. Timmreck, T. C. *Dictionary of Health Services Management*, 2d ed. Owings Mills, MD: National Health Publishing, 1987.
3. Brickner, W. H. and Cope, D. M. *The Planning Process*. Cambridge, MA: Winthrop Publishers, 1977.
4. Numerof, R. E. *The Practice of Management for Health Care Professionals*. New York: AMACOM, 1982.
5. Green, L. W. and Kreuter, M. W. *Health Promotion Planning:An Educational and Environmental Approach*, 2d ed. Mountain View, CA: Mayfield Publishing, 1991.
6. Alreck, R. L. and Settle, R. B. *The Survey Research Handbook*. Homewood, IL: Irwin, 1985.
7. Kerlinger, F. N. *Foundations of Behavioral Research*, 3d ed. New York: Holt, Rinehart & Winston, 1986.
8. Neale, J. M. and Liebert, R. M. *Science and Behavior*, 3d ed. Englewood Cliffs, NJ: Prentice-Hall, 1986.
9. Timmreck, T. C. *Study and Results of the Survey Conducted by the Cache County Independent Living Project (Area Wide Model Project)*. Logan (Cache County), UT, 1973.
10. Sherwood, R. W. *Box Elder County's Older Adults:An Assessment of Needs and Resources*. Brighton City, UT: Box Elder County Council on Aging Independent Living Project, 1973.

Chapter 6

Determining and Setting Priorities

THE ROMAN RULE
The one who says it cannot be done should never interrupt the one who is doing it.
MURPHY'S LAW[1]

CHAPTER OBJECTIVES

The main purposes of this chapter are to:

1. Present how to determine and identify barriers to services and programs.

2. Present how to ascertain what services and programs are functioning properly and how to determine what gaps in programming and service delivery exist.

3. Assist the planner in determining the pressing need for services and programs that can be provided.

4. Assist the planner in ascertaining if the organization can meet or develop the discovered needs as shown by the need assessment findings.

5. Use some methods and models to set priorities for program development determined by need assessment findings.

STEP 5

Determine and Set Priorities

- What are the major gaps in existing services and programs?

- In addition to the gaps in services, what are the all-important identified needs for services and programs that your organization can provide?

- Make decisions, ascertain needs, set priorities.

Barriers to Access of Health and Social Services

Barriers to accessibility of community health or social services can be physical, social, cultural, and/or economic. Poverty, lack of education, prejudice, and consumer attitudes are also barriers to services.

Physical barriers can be distance, access to transportation, and mobility—handicaps or disabilities are very real problems. Lack of wheelchair ramps, steps, or stairs; weather; waiting for a time for transportation; and long distances to walk are also physical barriers. Social barriers can be prejudice, socioeconomic status, pride, and group differences, all of which restrict access. Cultural beliefs, religion, folklore, personal health and medical practices, and fear of the organized service delivery system can contribute to some people's willingness to utilize community health and social services. The lack of finances, the need to prioritize spending limited funds, the inability to qualify for certain health or social services, the lack of insurance, and even not recognizing one's poverty status are related to the ability to acquire services. All of these are major economic barriers to obtaining adequate health and social services.

After considering the barriers to services mentioned above, the planner should evaluate potential barriers the target population may possess. As need assessment approaches are developed, barriers to the planned services should be anticipated and included in the methodologies—questionnaires, interviews, and the like.

Factors Influencing Priority Setting

How the people in a catchment area feel about health and social service problems is important to the planning process and should be considered. An array of special interests and opinions as to what are the best and needed services may be expressed by the people in the catchment area. Use the statistical findings from the need assessment process to determine the needs of the target population. The values and attitudes of people do matter in the end; if potential recipients of services do not support newly developed programs, the time, effort, and money spent developing a service are wasted, even if a need exists. If potential recipients develop a negative attitude toward the service, or toward the organization sponsoring the service, use of the service and support for it will be lacking.[2]

The planner has to achieve a consensus as to what the statistical findings of the need assessment represent. What are the perceived needs of the people in the community? A well-developed need assessment should be able to meet both statistical and perceived need issues. These should come together in the presentation of findings and in setting of priorities.

Priority determination is the process of imposing the values and expectations of the potential recipients onto the findings of the need assessment. The planner and program development professional has the responsibility of accomplishing this chore. Because need assessments tap into the opinion of people in the target population, the findings of the need assessment should represent the values and expectations of the community.

Priority setting, as used in a government agency or under a government contract, may be imposed on the community by the types of monies that are made available. The money, regulations, and guidelines attached to a government-funded project determine the types of programs to be developed and the direction they must go. Need assessments are conducted within the constraints set forth by the contract or the grant. If a need assessment is required under a grant or contract, the basic principles of need assessments presented in this book will be of value and useful. The restrictions in priority setting most likely will be determined by the guidelines and monies available for need assessment activities. The intended priorities of a hospital, a medical center, a health department, a social service agency, or other organization override findings of need assessments if the need assessments do not support its overall mission and goals.

Several entities have an interest in priority setting for program development: the recipient/patient, the sponsoring organization, the funding agency, the professional health care or service provider, and the community at large. Vested interests should be minimized from all parties.

Availability of money or the ability to make or attract money may be the final determining factor when it comes to program development or planning a project. Many health and social needs exist, but if no money exists to support or fund them, programs have a limited chance of being developed. Because program development monies are limited and scarce, priority setting is a very important process. The needs and areas that can be impacted the most should be attended to first; less important needs can be taken care of when resources eventually are sufficient to meet those needs. Therefore, priority setting is fundamental to program development—direct efforts in order to take care of the greatest needs first.

Priority Setting: Comparing Existing Resources, Services, and Gaps in Services

The first step in setting priorities is to analyze the findings of the need assessment. The minimum data analysis the planner should provide is a complete range of descriptive statistics, tables, charts, and graphs as set forth in Chapter 5. From percentages, rates, central tendencies, and other related data, the planner can determine the needs that the need

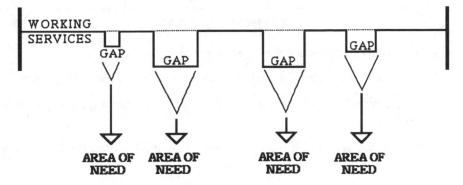

FIGURE 6.1. *Findings of Need Assessments Identify Gaps in Services*

assessment process uncovered. The next step is to clearly identify all existing services and programs available in the community or catchment area that are meant to meet these needs as found by the need assessment. The planner can determine quite quickly the areas of need that exist and whether the newly found needs are already being met in the community by reviewing the existing services operating in the catchment area. (See Figure 6.1.)

Determining the areas of need is a relatively simple and easy process. From the findings of the need assessment and assessment of the community services and resources, gaps and needs are easily identified. The difficulty is not to ascertain what the gaps in services are but to determine which gaps or needs are the most important and which have the greatest need. Determining which needed service to put money, time, effort, and resources into is the challenge. Prioritizing becomes the key and essential activity of the planner.

Prioritizing is a decision-making process. A two-phase process is required: a decision process and prioritizing process. A multitude of decision-making matrixes, models, and methodologies are at the disposal of the planner. Some decision-making models are complex, using quantitative and mathematical techniques. Other models are complex matrix approaches. Other decision-making models are more observational and use managerial decision-making approaches. The decision-making and prioritizing model the planner chooses often is based on the expertise and desired outcome of the organization and the circumstances at hand.

PLANNING QUESTIONS

☐ How many people does the need or problem impact?

☐ What will be the status or level of the problem in 5 years? 10 years?

☐ Left unfulfilled and unattended will this need or problem go away or solve itself?

☐ What is the extent of discomfort or inconvenience caused by this need not being met?

☐ How many disabled, immobile, or otherwise restricted persons are affected by this need not being filled?

☐ What is the level of community interest in this problem?

☐ Will this need, if met positively, affect the health status of the target population?

☐ What is the public and target population's attitude toward the perceived need(s)?

☐ What is the attitude of the administration toward efforts to fill the need and solve the problems identified in the need assessment?

Decision-Making Processes

Quantitative decision-making models are most useful in empirical research projects, where complex data sets and multiple levels of need exist, and where large financial commitments are involved. Matrix and managerial planning decision-making models are more commonly used by program development professionals and planners than complex statistically based approaches. Quantitative and statistically based approaches are most useful and effective, but use of them may be contingent on the planner's statistical expertise in their use. A more sophisticated statistical analysis of need assessment data is the best approach. However, if such expertise is lacking, other approaches do prove useful and will do the job. The results of the less complex decision-making and prioritizing models provide sufficient information and enough insight to make good planning and program development decisions.

Decision making is generally classified in two general categories: planning and managerial. Planning decisions are unique and innovative and require judgment and creativity. Quantitative tools become less useful in making program development decisions needed for the implementation process. Judgments about program development rely on ranking procedures and prioritizing systems. Quantitative tools are more useful in managerial decisions. Heuristic decision-making approaches—relating to exploratory problem-solving techniques that utilize self-educating techniques to improve performance and provide aid or direction in solving a problem—must take place with planning decisions, especially those that are innovative or pioneering in nature.[3]

The planner can use different types of decision-making approaches: empirical research, modeling, simulation, decision trees, and so on.[2] However, this book only focuses on the models that have two essential common elements. One is that the model is effective and reliable. Second, the model must be easy to comprehend and use, while producing the greatest amount of information with the least amount of effort—expediency being the more important value for the efficient planner.[3]

Approaches and Models

Decision Trees

The logical prioritizing process of need assessments can be accomplished with the help of a diagram called a decision tree. Once the need assessment is complete, and the data analysis is done, the planner can place the major gaps/needs in a decision tree, one at a time. (See Figures 6.2 and 6.3.)

The needs of a project being considered are represented by a "beginning box" that has several branches extending out from it. The branches lead to alternative courses of action. Example One: A hospital determines from a need assessment that it should develop a transportation system for the elderly (see Figure 6.2). The planner uses the decision tree to help decide whether to plan a minibus service for the elderly run by the organization or to contract with an existing service. Example Two: A hospital decides from a need assessment of all hospital employees that they need a comprehensive health promotion program to improve health status of the workers, improve morale, and reduce medical insurance premiums. One decision

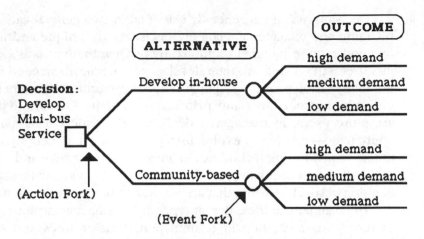

FIGURE 6.2. *Decision Tree—Need for a Mini-bus Transportation Service*

SOURCE: Adapted from Rowe et al., *Strategic Management.*[5]

branch would be to consider hiring a director to organize the project using in-house facilities and staff. A second decision tree branch (see Figure 6.3) would be to consider using an outside service with a contractual arrangement.

Alternative actions are presented and different directions or forks can be taken—called action forks. Some decision trees use simple

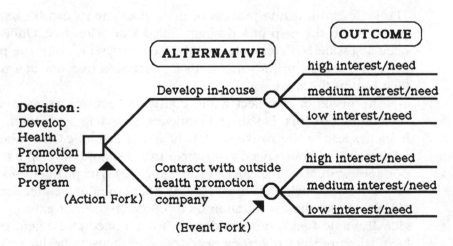

FIGURE 6.3. *Decision Tree—Need for an Employee Health Promotion Program*

SOURCE: Adapted from Rowe et al., *Strategic Management.*[5]

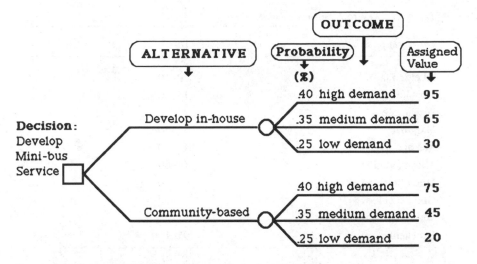

FIGURE 6.4. *Quantified Decision Tree with Assigned Values*

SOURCE: Adapted from Rowe et al., *Strategic Management.*[5]

"yes" or "no" action branches. Others provide direction as to what to consider next in both directions. (See Figures 6.2, 6.3, and 6.4.)[4,5]

After the action branches have been drawn, the planner considers how the events could affect the outcome of each *need* decision. The point at which an event or concern requires a new decision is termed an *event fork*. Event forks are the small circles. A planner might want to consider the demand for the service being planned at three levels of importance: high, medium, or low. Two, three, four or as many branches as needed are drawn and filled in according to the type of need being addressed and decision levels.[4,5]

Once the decision tree is drawn and filled in, the planner uses various considerations, points of concern, or issues as criteria to assess the outcomes of each need shown in the branches of the tree. Criteria can include: finances, demand for the service, its desirability, statistical findings of the need assessment, support of the administration of the organization, how great the need really is within the target group, how close other services or agencies come to filling this gap/need, potential for ongoing delivery of service, accessibility of the service, and so on.

Planning and program development often use nonmonetary criteria to ascertain a need for services. Need assessment data and other statistics should be used in the decision-making process. Because planning decisions need to be clearly set forth and understood, a scale

TABLE 6.1. *Key to Numbers of Figure 6.4*

Outcome possibility	Value
Likely to fail	0–10
Very low success	11–20
Low success	21–30
Marginal	31–40
Average	41–50
Above average	51–60
Much better than average	61–70
Good success	71–80
Very good success	81–90
Excellent	91–100

of values can be applied to decision trees to establish need outcomes. For example, "0 points" can be assigned to the least desirable outcome and "100 points" can be assigned to the most desirable outcome, with a complete range of possibilities assigned numbers in between 0 and 100 points. For example, after the minibus service is operational, the greatest outcome would be a very high demand for the service and then demand in the decision tree would be assigned 90 to 100. If there is little chance that the community-based transportation service will work, an 11 to 20 point range would be assigned. (See Figure 6.4 and Table 6.1.)

After the decision tree has been drawn and the value of each outcome has been defined, the planner determines the probability that each event will occur. For example, the planner assumes that there is a 40 percent chance of having a high demand, a 35 percent chance of having a medium demand, and only a 25 percent chance of having a low demand. The assigned value should add up to 100 percent.[5]

The planner has to decide which action establishes a high priority. To make the decision, a computation—the expected value of each action branch—is needed. Expected value is computed by multiplying the probability of occurrence (percent) and the assigned value of each outcome. The results of three separate computations (high, medium, low) are totaled. The percentages (probability) and assigned values (see Figure 6.4) are computed as follows:

$$(.40 \times 95) + (.35 \times 65) + (.25 \times 30) = 68.25$$
$$(.40 \times 70) + (.35 \times 45) + (.25 \times 20) = 50.75$$

Thus, the planner observes that the probability of success of operating the minibus service in-house is greater than that of a community-based service. The recommendation is to operate the minibus in-house. The risk in the decision depends on the amount of information available about each possible event. If additional information can be obtained and more accurate assigned values and probabilities can be arrived at, a better decision can be made.

Decision trees are good for defining the problem as well as assisting in solving the problem.[5] Some experts suggest that this type of decision tree is more useful in asking questions than in providing answers. No matter how much information is gained or how much one tries to quantify the decision, the planner and/or administration still has to make the decision and set the priorities.

Decision Tree: Another Model

As in the previously discussed decision tree approach, need has to be investigated before coming to a decision about setting priorities. If need is sufficient to warrant further analysis, the barriers to proceeding need to be reviewed and the various steps in decision making that pertain to the need to be addressed need to be considered.[4]

Any need or any phase of a need can be analyzed using the decision tree approach. Boxes with "yes" or "no" decision-making contingencies are drawn by the planner while asking key leading questions. The planner selects a gap/need and asks questions regarding all aspects related to administrative, social, and economic concerns. The questions must be able to be answered yes or no. With each yes or each no, an alternative action must be provided.

Figure 6.5 presents a decision tree approach using the need for elderly housing. Housing is used only as an example since any health promotion, health service, or social service need ascertained by the need assessment process and the planner can be plugged into a decision tree. The size and shape of the decision tree is determined by the number of questions to be answered, the specific details needed in

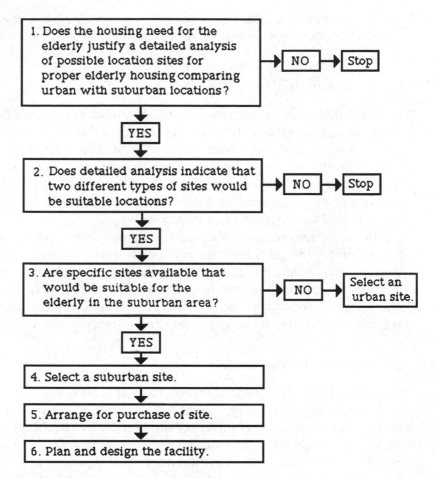

FIGURE 6.5. *Decision Tree—Elderly Housing Site Determination*

SOURCE: Adapted from Lawton et al., *Community Planning for an Aging Society.*[4]

answering the questions, and the number of steps required to complete the tree to arrive at the answer.

Matrix Decision-Making Models

Matrix decision-making models are used in a range of disciplines from health planning to epidemiology from health promotion to marketing. A decision-making matrix most often begins with the simple but effective "box matrix."[6,7] (See Figure 6.6.) The box structure allows the planner to determine four levels of importance for each decision. The planner simply draws a box and plugs the appropriate four levels of

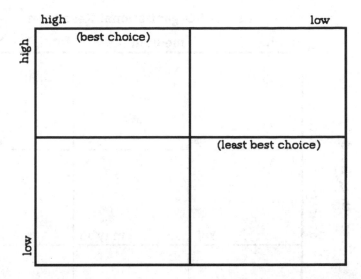

FIGURE 6.6. *Decision Matrix—A high/high decision is the best choice with a low/low being the least attractive choice.*

each decision into each cell. If a decision is needed between several services being considered, a matrix is drawn for each service. The same variables of comparison are presented in the matrix. When all comparisons are made, the matrix that is weighted the heaviest in the "high/high" box is the one selected.

The matrix or grid is used for decision making to set service priorities or program needs. The 4-cell grid as presented in Figure 6.6 is used to assist in general decisions. The 9-cell grid, as presented in Figure 6.7, allows for more input, more detail, and a more finely tuned decision. Levels of input are derived from two variables; nine elements of input are available to help make a decision.[6] The 9-cell grid can be used to compare a whole array of variables—one is compared to another. For example, in Figure 6.7, the importance of the "need" is compared to the resources available in the organization to meet the need. In Figure 6.1 four "gaps in services" were identified. The planner draws four different grids. In each grid, the planner places the different "gaps in service" on the left side of the grid and organizational resources at the top remain the same.

Planning questions about the grid are asked. For example, four different services were identified as needs and could be planned and implemented—transportation, a clinic at the senior citizen's center, health education for the elderly at a housing project, and a delivered meals program. They were identified within the catchment area,

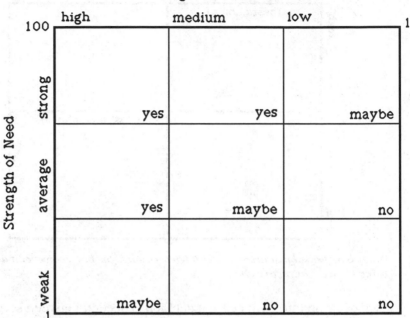

FIGURE 6.7. *Nine-Cell Decision Matrix*

therefore a 9-cell grid would be drawn for each of the four needs. Strengths are listed and given a number equal to their importance, ranging from 1 to 100. The same process is conducted for the weaknesses. This routine is used for resources of the organization as well. When the three "yes" cells are arrived at, either the planner can make an administrative decision about the priorities of the three "yes" cells, or new grids for the "yes" cells can be drawn and used to determine which of the three is the best decision. The final set of three grids produces a decision that would become the priority "need" to be addressed.

Setting Priorities of Needs

Priority determination should foster community participation for acceptance of the program and the service being planned. Priority setting links quantifiable data with the expectations of the community and the organization. Priority determination can be used for setting priorities from findings of the need assessment. Priority-setting processes are used to rank solutions to identified gaps and to select specific programs needed to achieve the goals and expectations of the organization. They also can be used to determine which goals are the most important.[2]

The Hanlon Method of Priority Setting

Three objectives underlie the Hanlon priority-setting method[2]:

- To permit the planner to identify major factors to be included in the priority-setting process.
- To organize the factors into groups that are weighted relative to each other.
- To allow the factors to be changed as needed.

Decision-making factors can be divided into four components. Each component is given a value to be used for scoring each factor on a predetermined scale. Components are inserted into two formulas that reflect the relative weight of each component.[2]

> Component A = size of the problem
> Component B = seriousness of the problem
> Component C = effectiveness of the solution
> Component D = P EA R L factors assessed

P EA R L is an acronym for a group of factors that are not directly related to actual need. P EA R L does help determine whether a program or service can be implemented and successful (Spiegel & Hyman, 1978).

> P = propriety
> E = economic feasibility
> A = acceptability
> R = resource availability
> L = legality

The following two formulas are used to insert the scores from the four components:

> Basic Priority Rating (BPR) = (A + B) C
> Overall Priority Rating (PR) = (A + B) C × D

TABLE 6.2. *Breakpoints and Scores for Determining Priorities Using Hanlon's Model*

Percentage of population affected	Score
Breakpoints	
75% or more	10
50% to 74%	8
25% to 49%	6
10% to 24%	4
Less than 10%	2

The planner must exercise good managerial and educated judgment related to the factors used in the priority-setting process. Relative weights assigned are based on the planner's perceived understanding of the need.

Components of Hanlon's Model

Component A. Size of the problem, that is, the number of persons affected by the problem or the number of persons in the catchment area needing the service. Once the estimated size is determined, the score corresponding to the size of the problem (see Table 6.2) is used as the value of that factor and is placed in the formula.

Component B. Seriousness of the problem, that is, a list of factors to be used in determining the seriousness of the problem is established by the planner. The list must be reasonable and realistic. The seriousness of the problem is determined by scoring each factor on a 0 to 10 scale, with 10 being the most serious. An average score is determined and an average score for components B is determined.

After a factor to be scored is defined, a table is developed that matches the factor to a score. The seriousness of a problem can be shown by the number or percentage of a population affected. The table could set forth percentages directly affected. Categories are set in the table. Breakpoints can be set arbitrarily but should not exceed 10. The groups should make up a large portion of the base figure. The highest breakpoint would be considered the most serious category.

Component C. Effectiveness of the solution, that is, how well can this problem be solved? Effective assessment is important, and to be able to use the formula, estimates are needed. The answer to the effectiveness of the solution is presented as an estimate. This component is scored within a range of .5 to 1.5. The low end of the range signifies that the program or service will not improve the need to the level required. The high end of the range, 1.5, represents a service level that is at or above the level desired to fill the gap/need and should be implemented. The 1.0 level is one of no commitment. The figure arrived at is inserted into the formula as C (component C). The values are tabulated to produce an average. This value is inserted into the formula.

Will not   ___ .5 ___ 75 ___ 1.0 ___ 1.25 ___ 1.5 ___ Will
                      No decision (neutral)

Component D. P E A R L factors assessed. This is a group of factors that are not directly related to the actual need found in the need assessment but are important to consider prior to implementation to ensure success. Each of the P E A R L factors is appraised by giving each a value of 0 to 1. Tables and grids can be used to set up complex sets of factors and data to use the Hanlon method and to derive the numbers to plug into the formulas.[2]

PLANNING QUESTIONS

☐ What level of priority setting and decision making does the current need assessment require?

☐ What general need(s) should be addressed?

☐ What specific "sub-needs" should be prioritized and are decisions about them needed?

☐ How complex of a decision or prioritizing approach is needed?

☐ If a decision-making model or matrix is to be used, which approach will be most effective given the data and circumstances at hand?

☐ Will the solution or decision truly solve the problem and fill the need?

☐ How accurate is the priority and will it solve the need assessment findings?

☐ Will the solution create other problems? If so, how major or minor?

☐ What is the attractiveness or aesthetic effect of the solution?

☐ Can this new program be coordinated with other programs and all other services in the continuum of services?

☐ Have the other solutions for filling the gap been seriously and thoroughly considered?

References

1. Bloch, A. *Murphy's Law Book Three*. Los Angeles: Price/Stern/Sloan, 1982.
2. Spiegel, A. D. and Hyman, H. H. *Basic Health Planning Methods*. Rockville, MD: Aspen Publishing, 1978.
3. Cone, P. R., Phillips, H. R., and Saliba, S. J. *Strategic Resources Management*, 1. Berrien Springs, MI: Andrew's University Press, 1986.
4. Lawton, M. P., Newcomer, R. J., and Byerts, T. O. *Community Planning for an Aging Society*. New York: McGraw-Hill, 1976.
5. Rowe, A. J., Mason, R. O., Dickel, K. E., and Snyder, N. H. *Strategic Management*. Reading, MA: Addison-Wesley, 1989.
6. Pearce, J. A. and Robinson, R. B., Jr. *Strategic Management*, 3d ed. Homewood, IL: Irwin, 1988.
7. Nutt, P. C. *Planning Methods for Health and Related Organizations*. New York: Wiley, 1984.

Chapter 7

How to Prepare for Implementation of Services: Getting Things Done

Whenever you set out to do something, something else must be done.

Every solution breeds new problems.

MURPHY'S LAW[1]

CHAPTER OBJECTIVES

The main purposes of this chapter are to:

1. Encourage the planner to consider and thoroughly ponder what needs to be accomplished in program implementation in detail and on a step-by-step basis.

2. Encourage the planner to review which activities precede other activities and what activities either have a priority for implementation or need to be accomplished first.

3. Review approaches to implementation including pilot projects, modified implementation approaches, and full implementation.

4. Review and assess all activities that need to be accomplished in order to implement the project in detail.

5. Provide a list of considerations and planning questions that will assist the planner and administration in implementing the project.

STEP 7

Step-by-Step Activities and Procedures

- What needs to be done first? What needs to be done before other activities can take place?

- What items or processes need to be in place before others can start?

Pilot Projects

- Should a pilot project be developed and implemented prior to committing to a full-blown project? Is a pilot project a logical approach for the project at hand?

- Does the organization have the time and resources for a pilot project?

- Would a pilot project be a waste of time, money, and resources, and therefore should it not be considered? Would a pilot project be a good alternative, and should a pilot project be planned?

Some Things to Consider

- Purchase of equipment and supplies.

- Office space acquired and set up.

- Hiring of personnel.

- Agreements and contracts formally made.

- Legal aspects considered and dealt with.

- Budgets developed.

- Accounting and budget management systems developed.

- Policies and procedures set forth.

- Marketing and community education developed.

- Staffing and organizational structure, meetings, and reporting systems in place.

- Coordination, organization, supervision, and communication systems developed.

- Plans for growth, expansion, and development.

- Forms and paperwork processes developed.

Setting Activities in Order

One of the most challenging activities surrounding planning and implementing a new project is to get all details of each activity worked out. It is a challenge to mentally think through each phase, step, and activity to ascertain which should come first, which activities rely on others being finished, which activities can be done independently of others, and so on. Often it is obvious which activities need to be done and which come first. Yet, some activities to be accomplished and the order in which they are to occur is not always so obvious. Certain activities cannot be started, let alone accomplished, without other more basic activities being in place.

A somewhat graphic example is that of the construction of a house. One cannot put up the studs for the walls and cover them with Sheetrock and later decide to put in the wiring for the electricity, phone, TV cables, and pipes for plumbing. Practicality requires the pipes and wires to go in as soon as the studs are in place, before anything else is done. If not, the Sheetrock wall covering would end up with holes punched in it; the result would be quite a mess. So it goes for the implementation of health promotion and social and health services projects. The order in which certain activities should be put in place can be as obvious as the construction process mentioned here.

Opening a clinic for older adults may involve opening offices and even construction or remodeling of a building for the clinic and offices. Starting up a health promotion program may include lining up special screening equipment and having facilities for offices, health counseling, large rooms for group fitness programs, and the like. The planner would not want to kick off a major media and advertising phase of a project, announcing the opening when the office has not yet been opened, or the project even officially approved. Nor would the administrators want to order letterhead stationery and envelopes with addresses on them when the site for the new project is not yet finalized. Thus, certain things have to be accomplished, completed, or in place before other things can be done. It is the job of the planner to mentally walk through every detail—all of the steps and activities that need to be done to implement a project—and determine the order of each activity.

Activities and Procedures Planning Protocol Document

Some planners develop a major planning document that details each and every minute activity to be accomplished for this phase of the planning process and the various sets of activities and procedures. This document is not the program plan but an implementation planning protocol that spells everything out.

The key to successful use of an *activities and procedures planning protocol document* comes through the assignment of responsibility for all activities. Each activity should have one person (and only one) named as the sole responsible individual selected to ensure its completion.

Some activities are not contingent on others being in place and can easily be completed while waiting for the step-by-step process to occur. Ascertaining activities that can be done while waiting for the slower processes to be completed is good time management. The planner should not wait for small, unrelated, or trivial activities to be finished when separate or different major activities that are not contingent on a step-by-step process could be completed.

Team effort in the planning process should include administrators, health promotion professionals, clinicians, professional staff, and any workers or personnel involved. Brainstorming sessions and other related planning meetings should include all personnel involved, not just administration or planners.

- Secretaries should be included in planning their workstations
- Nurses and physicians should help plan patient flow or treatment stations
- Business office personnel should help plan the billing forms
- Health educators should be involved in planning educationally related facilities
- Health promotion personnel should provide input into screening structure and flow
- Medical records personnel should be included in medical record form development, record flow systems, and storage and retrieval of records

When one phase of a program or one department will interact with another and be dependent on any other programs or departments, an overt effort should be made to invite the appropriate members of those departments and programs to planning meetings.[2]

Pilot Projects

Pilot projects are defined in several ways. They can be test cases or a dry run of a program in which little knowledge or experience exists. The pilot project is done to see how things will go. It also can be a modified and simplified run of a project prior to implementing a full-blown project. A pilot project could be a shortened version of the main project that is fully implemented but is not a fully involved approach. Usually pilot projects are done to save money and resources and in some cases reduce risk.

A pilot project also can be the first program or service to be implemented in a series of similar projects. For example, if one were to open several health promotion clinics in a few senior apartment complexes, only one clinic would be opened and fully implemented at one site. The process, administration, effectiveness, efficiency, flow of work, use of personnel, physical structure of equipment and furniture would all be evaluated. Bugs and shortcomings could be worked out and corrections made. These trial-run type activities take place prior to further commitment of money and resources. Evaluation activities would be completed prior to opening clinics at other sites.

Some projects are too costly or too risky for total financial, personnel, resources, and time commitment without knowing if the concept is sound and if the system will work. Thus, administrators may wish a trial run instead of implementing the total project. Educated observation, research, and practical experience has shown that the conservative approach may be a wise one. Yet, it also has been shown that the conservative approach can set up new programs for failure. Planners often plan for success and do so with a fairly conservative use of resources.

Step 7 of the Planning Model asks "Does the organization have the time and resources for a pilot project?" The first response to this question by any administrator would be, "Why? Everyone knows it is less costly to implement a pilot project than a full-blown one." Initially and on the surface, this appears to be a true statement. However, over the long haul in health promotion and social and health services, it may be more costly to modify a well-planned project developed over many months into a pilot project than to implement it as a full-blown project. Changing a major project into a half-baked pilot project, especially after extensive commitments and resources have been put into planning activities, may cause the organization and administration to pay for the last-minute change later. The losses could be in long-term costs which eventually have to be paid out, plus the planning cost, as well as loss of job satisfaction, discouragement, and loss of confidence in the administration by the planner and staff and the organization's employees.

Administrators have been known (more often than many are willing to admit) to take good planning and program it for failure by implementing well-developed projects as pilot projects or modified versions of the planned project. Such moves are a waste of time, money, effort, and morale and destroy the commitment of the planners. Such approaches defeat the entire planning process. Administrators need to be cautioned about such self-defeating acts.

If pilot projects are to be used, they should be a part of the initial planning process; they should be discussed at the beginning of planning discussions. Pilot projects should not be just an afterthought by administrators in order to conserve money or take a less costly approach at the last minute prior to implementation, especially after a major planning effort that has expended a fair amount of time and resources.

Even though some modified, shortened, less expensive pilot project approaches have succeeded, most have not and often shortchange any possibility for program success.

If a good need assessment has been conducted, what needs to be accomplished should be quite clear. The assessment may show how much the program is needed, and if it will be successful. With a good need assessment completed and the results studied, a full-blown approach should be justified. Full implementation of a health promotion program or a needed social or health service is the preferred and most effective approach.

Approaches to Determine Step-by-Step Procedures

One approach found useful in determining those activities which should be done and which activities have to be accomplished prior to others being done is the decision tree as described in Chapter 6. Another approach to determining which activities to put into action is an activity planning matrix. (See Figure 7.1.)

Using the Planning Matrix

The most important activities and/or those needing to take place first are listed in the upper left-hand corner of the matrix. Those that need to be done first are listed in the left-hand (1st) column starting at the top. Items related to a particular activity that is to occur second are listed in the second column. High-priority, second-stage items are listed at the top. Items related to a particular activity needing to occur third are listed in the third column, and so forth. The same holds true for the fourth, fifth, sixth, or however many columns that are required. If additional related activities of one particular activity are needed, columns are added. Top-priority, first-stage activities are listed at the top of column one, top-priority, second-stage activities are listed in column two, and so on. Activities at the bottom of the matrix should be less essential than those at the top of each stage/column. On the other hand, bottom right activities may be listed last and only seem least important, but are essential though they are to be done last. All activities should be assigned to one person. Responsibility should rest on only one person who is to follow all assigned activities through to completion.

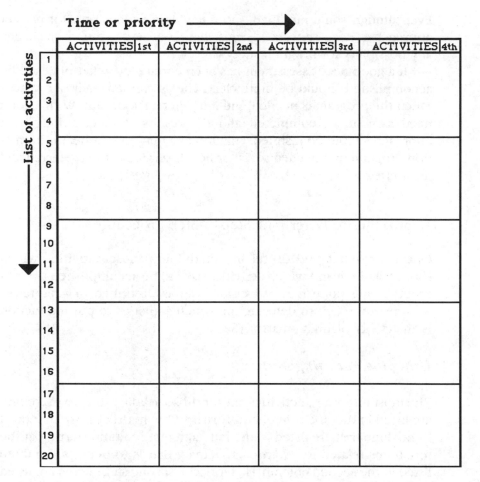

FIGURE 7.1. *Step-by-Step Activity Planning Matrix*

Levels of Importance of Activities

The planner and administrator both need to keep in mind that a small number of factors are responsible for a large amount of work and for the final results. For example, 15 percent of volunteers do 100 percent of the work or 10 percent of drivers cause 95 percent of the accidents. This is referred to as *Pareto's Law*. This law should be considered when determining which levels and activities are given the most attention and resources. The concept behind this law is that all things are not equally important. On the other hand, do not ignore minor things due to the dominance of the major issues. Some programs, activities, and personnel have more impact on the planning and implementation process than others. The greater the number of events included in the plan, the more complicated it may become; thus, the harder it is to keep track of the progress of each event and the overall project. Some activities have higher priorities than others, yet less significant activities also are essential and must not be overlooked. Good organization and coordination may rely on the small as well as large factors; thus all activities must be completed.[2]

PLANNING QUESTIONS

☐ Should a pilot project be considered?

☐ Should a full-blown project be implemented?

☐ Should the time, resources, and finances needed to implement a pilot project be expended or would it be more effective to use the money, time, and resources to go ahead with the full project?

☐ What would be the long-term effect and consequences of starting with only part of the project instead of the full project?

☐ Are pilot project considerations a part of the original discussions and planning efforts by both administration and planners?

☐ Is a pilot project really the best approach for the program being considered?

☐ Have the overall ramifications of a pilot project been considered and compared with implementation of a full-fledged project?

☐ If a pilot project approach is being considered, is it because it is preplanned and is from effective administrative decisions or is it a last-minute shortcut to save money and resources?

☐ Which 10 to 20 percent of the planning process should be given the most attention and resources?

☐ Are any activities being ignored or overshadowed by more dominant issues?

References

1. Bloch, A. *Murphy's Law and Other Reasons Why Things Go Wrong!* Los Angeles: Price/Stern/Sloan, 1977.

2. Brickner, W. H. and Cope, D. M. *The Planning Process.* Cambridge, MA: Winthrop Publishers, 1977.

3. Spiegel, A. D. and Human, H. H. *Basic Health Planning Methods.* Rockville, MD: Aspen Publishing, 1978.

Chapter 8

Developing Timelines for Planning and Implementation

Everything takes longer than you think.
Murphy's Law[1]

CHAPTER OBJECTIVES

The main purposes of this chapter are to:

1. Understand the use and function of timelines.

2. Understand how to use timeline charts in the planning process.

3. Understand the importance of the use of timelines in the planning and program development process

including use in implementation of programs.

4. Learn how to develop and construct timeline charts.

5. Present examples of timeline charts used in planning and program development.

STEP 8

Develop Timeline Charts

- Create and develop Timeline charts from the step-by-step activities and other matters that need to be accomplished.

Time in Planning and Implementation

A worker's level of responsibility often is reflected by the amount of time that worker will spend on planning and implementation. The higher the position and level of responsibility, the more time one spends on planning unless the person works solely as a planner. As Figure 8.1 shows, top administrators spend a great deal of time planning and less time on implementation. Middle managers have a moderate to heavy commitment to both planning and implementation. Workers carry out many of the implementation activities, but do little in the way of planning. Administrators are responsible for the overall planning and management of the organization. The time of a top administrator should be spent on the general and broad view of the organization, planning, and overall direction. The middle managers need to be involved in the activities of day-to-day operations and in program development, and they also are involved with the details of implementation.

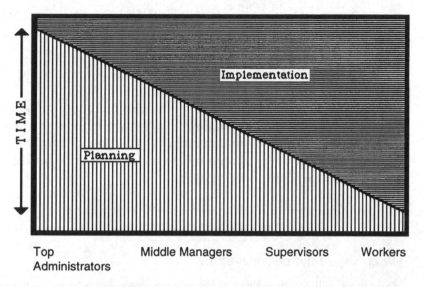

FIGURE 8.1. *Levels of Responsibilities and Amount of Time Involved in Planning and Implementation by Different Levels of Workers*

Time: Its Determination and Use

Time is a fundamental part of planning objectives; it is important in determining activities, implementation, and evaluation. Time, as used in timelines, can be stated in days, weeks, months, or years. The planner should take the kind of activity to be done into account in relation to the time needed for it to be implemented and completed. Separate timelines for daily, weekly, and monthly based activities and implementation can be developed. It is most common for the planner to choose week-based or month-based timelines. However, the planner could consider developing weekly as well as monthly timelines (if useful and appropriate). Short-term (daily) or long-term (yearly) timelines, in some cases, are also useful such as tracking grant cycles, opening a major facility, or overall strategic planning.

Timelines are guidelines and need to be flexible and modifiable. The planner should do his or her best to accurately predict time expectations for each activity. As work progresses, time frames change. Plans do not always go as well as they should; thus, timelines may need to be reassessed and changed to meet more realistic time frames. When writing objectives with time conditions included, great care must be taken to ensure that time frames or time expectations are not unduly inhibiting, limiting, or unreasonable.[2]

Timelines Described

Timelines often are presented as a modified form of a bar graph, providing a pictorial representation of activities in relation to various time elements: how long each activity will last, when the activity should begin, when it should end, whether it is an ongoing activity that occurs throughout the project.

PLANNING QUESTIONS

☐ When should the activities start?

☐ How long will the activities take to complete; how long will it run?

☐ When should the activity be finished? (Note it says "should," indicating predictions are not always easy to make and timelines should be flexible.)

Three of the greatest values timelines have added to the planning process are: (1) they cause the planner to list all key activities, (2) they require the planner to ascertain the time frame in which activities are to be performed, and (3) the planner has to determine an order of occurrence for events and activities.

Determining Priorities of Activities for Timelines and Implementation

One of the first chores of a planning staff is to identify the activities and constraints that affect implementation. Positive and negative issues and factors are considered, as are any constraints on the length of time needed to implement each activity. The planner also considers various time dimensions and tries not to overlook any one event or give too much emphasis to one area or activity. Adjustments are made for each activity in terms of time frames to achieve planning objectives. All factors—budgets, construction efforts, scientific understanding, hiring and staffing, purchasing of equipment and supplies, licensing, regulatory matters, approval from administration, funding sources, approval from government agencies, and so on—need to be considered. Common sense, clear and obvious observations, and preestablished criteria must be used to set and determine the priorities of timeline activities.[3]

One criterion that should be considered is whether certain objectives require more time than others to achieve. If time alone is used as the criterion for determining priorities, then inaccurate decisions on implementation priorities may result. A multitude of factors place time constraints on the implementation of projects.[3] For example, as a planner moves to open an outpatient clinic for older adults, he or she may find that it cannot move in until the clinic is inspected and approved by a fire marshal. What may determine timeline completion is not how quickly one can paint and move furniture in, but how soon compliance with regulations can be met—how soon the fire marshal will come to inspect the facility and grant approval.

Developing Timelines

Timeline Basics

The following should be included in all timelines, regardless of their presentation:

- Use a pictorial or graphic presentation format.
- List all major activities and the time frame in which each is to take place and be completed.
- Provide a continuum of time that can be referred to—i.e., days, weeks, months, or years.
- Set the timeline up in a manner that will indicate where the activity should be at a certain time and so it can be seen easily on the chart.

Several approaches have been developed to determine short-term and long-term planning time frames. Simple timelines are basic to planning and program development and have been used to help plan work and implement new projects for some time. One of the first timeline systems to be formalized was the Gantt Chart.

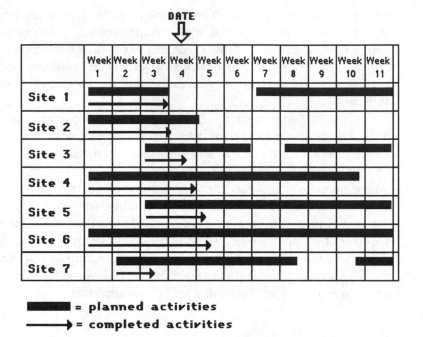

FIGURE 8.2. *Gantt Chart—Management of a Health Promotion Program for the Older Adults in a Retirement Community*

Gantt Chart

Figure 8.2 shows an effective time planning tool that has proven useful in determining what time frames it takes to complete certain tasks or activities. The rows on the left of the chart represent individual phases or activities. The time schedule is subdivided into appropriate time units of either hours, days, or weeks across the top. The Gantt Chart is based on action—doing, getting projects or activities done. A heavy horizontal line is drawn in each row (across) to show the amount of time each person, project, or activity needs to complete the task. As work proceeds, a lighter line is drawn next to the heavy line. The lighter line shows actual progress: how far into the project the work has been completed; to what extent, timewise, things have been accomplished. A vertical marker in the form of an arrow indicates the current date.[4]

The administrator or planner is to update the chart weekly. If the chart is kept current, the administrator or planner can see the project's progress at a glance. With a quick glimpse at the chart, the administrator knows if the project is ahead of schedule, right on schedule, or behind.

Gantt Charts are helpful when little or no relationship or interdependency among projects or activities exists. If an activity is not related to other activities, the administrator can tell how well it is doing in relation to the other parts or phases of the project. If an activity is connected to or dependent on another activity, then the administrator can quickly see whether it is on time or if it is causing a delay. When many different activities are to be conducted for one project, several Gantt Charts can be developed—one chart for each activity could be developed. These could be compared with each other to check progress and coordinate the various activities.[4]

PERT Charts

PERT Charts can be used as a timeline planning tool (see Figure 8.3). Like Gantt Charts, they have been used for some time as a planning tool. The PERT Chart approach to timelines has many of the same dimensions of other timeline approaches. That is, the chart consists of a diagram that presents the sequence of activities which need to be completed to ensure the implementation of a project or program.

The PERT Chart is not used as often by planners in health promotion, social or health-care services as it is by the military, the aerospace industry, and major high-tech corporations. The reason the PERT Chart approach is not used as often by health and social service planners is due to its complexity—there is a certain amount of quantitative analysis to it and a list of specialized terms and symbols. Overall PERT Charts are much more quantitative because such levels of specificity are required by engineering-type entities.[4,5]

As presented here, the PERT Chart timeline is a very basic and a modified approach; this is a simplified form compared to that used in engineering and other technology-driven industries. The planner is encouraged to develop and expand the basic chart to meet her or his planning needs and to use its capability to its maximum extent, based on the needs of the project and the planner's comfort level in quantitative approaches.

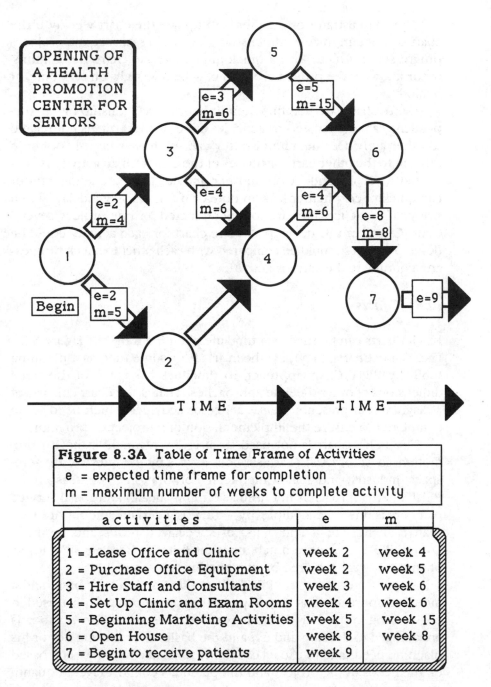

OPENING OF
A HEALTH
PROMOTION
CENTER FOR
SENIORS

T I M E — T I M E

Figure 8.3A Table of Time Frame of Activities

e = expected time frame for completion
m = maximum number of weeks to complete activity

activities	e	m
1 = Lease Office and Clinic	week 2	week 4
2 = Purchase Office Equipment	week 2	week 5
3 = Hire Staff and Consultants	week 3	week 6
4 = Set Up Clinic and Exam Rooms	week 4	week 6
5 = Beginning Marketing Activities	week 5	week 15
6 = Open House	week 8	week 8
7 = Begin to receive patients	week 9	

FIGURE 8.3. *Basic PERT Chart*

Rules for PERT Chart Development and Use

• The time frame moves from left to right.

• Numbered circles are called *events.*

• An *event* is a point in time at which some activity is to be completed.

• *Arrows* are activities that connect events and must be performed in order for an event to occur.

• Events do not occur until all work connected to and leading up to that event has been completed.

• The series of events, connected by arrows from beginning to end of the time frame, are called *paths* (see Figure 8.3 and Table 8.1).[4,5]

The PERT Chart Has Two Parts

Part 1. As shown in Figure 8.3, circles are *events.* Arrows are *activities.* To use the PERT Chart (see Figure 8.3), you always start with #1. The chart shows that activity #1 has to be completed before event #2 can happen. Activity #4 has to be completed before event #6 can happen, and so forth. A time frame is set forth and determined by an accompanying Table of Activities and time for completion (see Figure 8.3A). The activities in the table guide the planner through the PERT Chart to the ending date. The end date needs to be determined at the beginning of the planning process.[4,5]

Part 2. To be able to complete a project on time, using the PERT Chart, one needs to know a final or projected end date. The beginning date is "e" (e = time estimates of earliest time to begin). Each activity (arrow) can have a time frame as indicated on each (m = the latest date the event can take place). Thus, the simple approach to the chart has an "e" time and an "m" time, allowing for some time frame flexibility (see Figure 8.3).

In their simplest form, PERT Charts can be used with the above information. As used in aerospace, manufacturing, and high-tech industries, however, PERT Charts have been taken to complex levels and incorporate mathematical formulas to assist in analysis.[4,5] This book will not expand PERT charting to this level. Should a planner need a higher level of information, the use of PERT charting can be found in many management and planning textbooks and should be sought out.

Timelines

Gantt Charts, and PERT Charts, because of their complexity, are often avoided. The PERT Chart provides in-depth and specific details if developed to their fullest. Most planners do not feel the need for this level of complexity, however. Others believe that if PERT Charts are used, planners spend more time developing and managing the chart than they do the project. That is, the PERT Chart becomes a busy distraction with more effort expended on the activity of charting than on planning, program development, implementation, and evaluation.

Several timelines for general use are easy to understand and simple to construct. For the most part simpler timelines may fill the needs of most projects. The basics of timeline construction are:

1. Listing of activities;
2. Ascertaining which activities need to be done first;
3. Determining how long each activity will take (both time span and time frame);
4. Determining when each and every activity is to begin;
5. Determining when the activity should be finished, repeated, or in place;
6. Establishing what kind of time frame (i.e., weeks, months, years) is to be used;
7. Determining how to put items 1 through 6 above into picture form so they can be studied, reviewed, and tracked to see whether projects are ahead of schedule, on schedule, or behind schedule.

Figure 8.4 presents a timeline used to plan a nutrition program for a congregate. This example presents the short-term time frame items at the top of the chart and then works down the list of activities using a different type of bar format for each activity.

The planner's first task is to list, in the far left column, all the activities to be completed and prioritize those to be done first. The next step

ACTIVITIES	month	1	2	3	4	5	6	7	8	9	10	11	12
Purchase materials for service		▓												
Publicity & Public relations for opening/serve first meal. Coordination & arrangements for first meal at Center #1. Begin coordination and arrangements for Center #2. Complete arrangements for meal preparation. Clear project for food stamps Clear kitchen with Public Hlth. Coordinate transportation for bulk food. Hire personnel.		▓	▓											
Serve 1st meal at Center #1. (1st day of the month)		▓												
Publicity & coordination for Services at Center #2 & #3.		▓	▓											
Serve 1st meal at Center #2. (15th of the Month)		▓												
Serve 1st meal at Center #3. Publicity and coordination for service to Center No.4.		▓	▓	▓	▓									
Publicity & coordination for service to Center No.5. Serve 1st meal at Center #4.		▓	▓	▓	▓	▓								
Serve 1st meal at Center #5. Expand and serve meals as need and demand indicates.		▓	▓	▓	▓	▓	▓	▓	▓					
Conduct evaluation last meal of the month at each center. Evaluation-continual/monthly.		▓	▓	▓	▓	▓	▓	▓	▓	▓	▓	▓	▓	

SITES	
Center # 1	City Civic Center
Center # 2	Junior High Cafeteria
Center # 3	National Guard Armory
Center # 4	Hospital Cafeteria
Center # 5	Church Activity Hall

FIGURE 8.4. *Timeline for Implementation of Five New Congregate Meal Sites*

is to present the time frame as shown across the top of the figure—here it's in months. Actual dates can be used initially or added once they are determined. A bar is drawn for each activity to represent the period of time needed to complete them. For example, the fourth bar down in Figure 8.4 is for "Publicity and coordination for services at

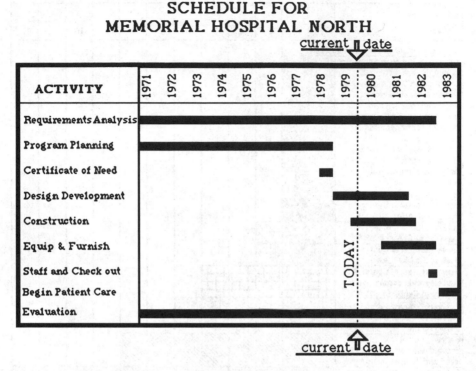

FIGURE 8.5. *Sample Timeline for Opening of a Hospital*

Centers #2 and #3." This is to start at the beginning of the project and be fully implemented by the end of the third month. The figure is from an actual plan used for the development and implementation of nutrition programs for a county aging program. One problem with this timeline chart is that it fails to account for the fact that all activities do not start at the same time nor does each activity start at the beginning of the project. Figure 8.5 accounts for this difference in the starting times of various activities.

Timelines of General Use

An adaptation of Figure 8.5 can be used for long-range planning. This figure presents a timeline used for the planning, development, construction, and the opening of a second hospital in a two-hospital system. The same basic approach, as presented in Figure 8.4 is used—that is, the activities are listed on the left column, the time frame is shown across the top. The differences between Figure 8.4 and Figure 8.5 are: (1) the time frame is in years, (2) the activities are quite general, and (3) the bars are presented in a broken fashion that is not attached to the left line. One problem with this timeline is that the activities are very general, vague, and fail to indicate where one is in the implementation process, as seen in the Gantt Chart.

For timelines to be effective, the activities should be as specific as can be ascertained. A major advantage of this approach (Figure 8.5) is that it more clearly indicates when the activity is to begin. Figure 8.4 leads one to believe that all activities will begin at once. From a practical point of view, common sense suggests this is not so. Some activities do begin at the very beginning; others begin midway into the project. Some activities may be very short lived and others are continuous. Figure 8.5 shows the beginning, length, and end of each activity more clearly. A line also is placed on the chart to indicate where the planning effort is on the current date. This figure is an adaptation from an actual certificate of need for development of a hospital. The hospital is now open and operating.

The sample timeline presented in Figure 8.6 titled "Timeline for Health Promotion Research Project" is si milar to Figure 8.5. The rules

Timeline for Health Promotion Research Project

	Month											
	1	2	3	4	5	6	7	8	9	10	11	12
Recruit and finalize co-researchers	x	x	x									
Finalize the development of questionnaire	x	x	x									
Training and instructions			x									
Contact hospitals				x	x	x	x	x				
Finalize visitation and interview plans				x	x	x	x	x				
Visitations and interviews				x	x	x	x	x				
Gather data and post visitation interviews									x	x		
Compile and analyze data									x	x	x	x
Write rough draft and develop report										x	x	x
Final draft of report printed												x
Assessment, feedback, and upgrading of project	x	x	x	x	x	x	x	x	x	x	x	x
Evaluation											x	x

FIGURE 8.6. *Actual Sample—General Use Timeline*

presented before for the development of timelines apply to this one as well. This example is from a grant for a research survey of rural hospitals. In this figure, the activities were first listed down the left column, time frames were decided on (months in this case), and time of beginning and completion were presented using "X" instead of bars for expediency in development.

The sample timeline presented in Figure 8.7 is similar to the examples shown in Figures 8.5 and 8.6. This timeline is used by a community health services agency to track and manage several programs that have been implemented. This agency had numerous contracts and projects that were hard to track. Thus, the executive director developed the timeline chart in Figure 8.7 to clearly present, in picture form, when each project began, how long it will run, and when it will end. As a management tool, timelines allow the administrator to effectively anticipate the end of a grant or contract, know what is required to complete the project, how much time is left to finish tasks, and anticipate when the money will run out.

Each project has its own uniqueness and approaches. Some projects will have multiple activities and multiple outcomes. Figure 8.8 is an example of how a multiple activity timeline can be constructed (unlike Figure 8.9, which shows how timelines can be within documents). Immunization clinics are often held at several sites. Usually different teams of clinicians are sent to different sites; clinics are repeated and have to be planned and tracked. The goal of the project example in Figure 8.8 is to hold 180 clinics at six different sites. These clinics all have to be completed within 15 months. Each and every clinic is assigned a number and a set of clinics are assigned to each team. Thus, "Team 1" will hold clinics 1 through 30, "Team 2," will hold clinics 31 through 60, and so forth. The clinics are to be put into action and completed in five phases. The "phase" part of the project allows for planning, management, and monitoring the clinics' progress toward meeting their goal. Because herd immunity is about 85 percent, this program will have to develop a follow-up to ensure those persons missed will get immunizations. The clinic manager has the responsibility for conducting follow-up and feedback, which is used to track people who have failed to be immunized. Follow-up clinics would be held and another timeline would be developed to monitor the clinics' activities.

```
                    TIMELINE OF CURRENT STATE CONTRACTS    JANUARY 1991

              1990                           1991
              JULY AUG SEPT OCT NOV DEC      JAN FEB MAR APR MAY JUNE JULY AUG SEPT OCT NOV DEC

EARLY INTERVENTION (**)
7/90 to 9/91                   **********************************************************  ---- ---- ---- ----
    191,833.00     |Beginning of 5th year

E.I. DEMONSTRATION PROJECT
1/90 to 9/91                                 ************************************************
     40,000.00                               |New Contract

HICAP (**)
7/90 to 6/91        *********************************************  ---- ---- ---- ---- ---- ----
    182,174.00     |Beginning of 3rd year

PEAK PERFORMANCE (*)
9/90 to 6/91          ***************************************  ---- ---- ---- ----
     46,757.00     |New Contract building upon 10 years previous contracts for Hypertension Control Program.

TOBACCO EDUCATION & CONTROL
A. CHURCH-BASED (STATE) (**)
7/90 to'12/91       **********************************************************************************************
    150,000.00     |New Contract

B. CHURCH-BASED (COUNTY SUB-CONTRACT) (**)
9/90 TO 8/91          ********************************************  ---- ---- ----
     31,100.00     |New Contract

C. VOCATIONAL SCHOOL-BASED (STATE)
1/1/91 TO 12/31/92                           ********************** * * (Two Year Grant)
    185,000.00                               |New Contract

TOTAL 826,914.00
(*) This is a three year grant which is reviewed by the state each year and refunded based on availability of funds.
(**) These four grants have a high probability of being refunded.
```

FIGURE 8.7. *Sample Timeline to Manage Contracts*

SOURCE: From an Inland Counties Health Systems Agency project, Riverside, California, 1991. Used with permission.

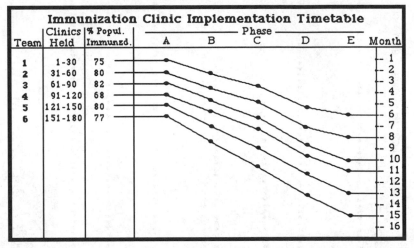

COUNTY PUBLIC HEALTH DEPARTMENT
IMMUNIZATION CLINIC PLAN

FIGURE 8.8. *Sample Timeline for Operation of Immunization Clinics*

Timelines can be a separate chart or can be incorporated into a working document which includes the basics of a project—i.e., objectives and individual activities to be conducted. Figure 8.9 presents a separate work plan with a separate page for each major phase. (Page 1 presents activity "A"—the development phase; page 3 presents activity "B"—site development.) Each program or project will have as many work plan sheets as is needed for each activity or phase.

The timeline in Figure 8.9 is presented in the far right column—activities are listed and time frames for each are determined. The overall time frame for this document is a yearly time period broken down into quarters. (See also Figures 8.10 and 8.11.)

A code is used to indicate the different quarters:

1st quarter = 1Q
2nd quarter = 2Q
3rd quarter = 3Q
4th quarter = 4Q

Activities are set to occur in one or more quarters. The timeline is determined by placing the code (i.e., 2Q, or 1Q-2Q) at the appropriate quarter within the timeline. Some codes are presented separately to indicate that the activity is to take place only in that one quarter. Other codes are connected by a line indicating that the activity is to occur over several quarters and in some cases several years. (See page 1, activity 3, which shows an example—volunteer recruitment is to occur over two-and-one-half years.)

Other Sample Timelines

Figure 8.10 is a sample timeline for strategic planning for a hospital. It is based on a one-year format using months as the time frame in which it will function. The activities that are continual and ongoing are indicated by two-headed arrows.

Figure 8.11 is a sample timeline for the implementation of Medicare preventive health services for the elderly. Triangles, circles, and squares are used to indicate the activities. The timeline is presented at the bottom of the chart and is on a four-year time frame. This timeline chart fails to clearly set out specific activities, and it does not indicate where the process is in the completion of the time frame. Clearer and more specific activities and when each should occur would enhance the value of this timeline approach.

PLANNING QUESTIONS

☐ Is there a clear understanding of and a list of implementation activities?

☐ Has a timeline chart approach that will be effective for the current project been selected?

☐ Which type of timeline/chart will work best for the current project and situation?

☐ Is the current project to be implemented in weeks, months, years?

☐ Have activities been set up in order of implementation and time of occurrence, and have they been listed in the proper sequence?

☐ Are the time frames realistic and possible to complete as expected?

☐ Has evaluation and feedback been included as part of the timeline?

State of California—Health and Welfare Agency
CONTRACT NO. _____

PROJECT WORKPLAN

Department of Health Services
EXHIBIT
Page __1__ of __11__

(Agency Name)   Inland Counties Health Systems Agency
(Project Title)   Inland Counties Hypertension Control Program
(Project Period)   07/01/87 To 06/30/90

The Contractor shall work toward achieving the project goals by accomplishing the following outcome objectives and activities. This shall be done by performing the specified activities and evaluating the results using the methods identified on "Project Workplan – Evaluation Plan" Form.

GOAL STATEMENT: To reduce the mortality and morbidity rates due to uncontrolled hypertension by identifying individuals with hypertension and assisting them to obtain and adhere to a treatment regimen.

COMPONENT I. Patient Adherence Through the TAKE CHARGE PROGRAM

MEASURABLE OUTCOME OBJECTIVES	IMPLEMENTATION ACTIVITIES	ACTIVITIES TIME LINE FISCAL YEARS			
		FY 1987/88	FY 1988/89	FY 1989/90	
OUTCOME OBJECTIVE I:	**ACTIVITY A:**				
At the end of three years 300 individuals (diagnosed as hypertensive or with an elevated BP reading) will have become a part of the TAKE CHARGE of your life PROGRAM. Of the 300, 100 (33%) will complete a referral to a physician and 150 (50%) will achieve a controlled BP (<140/90 or as defined by physician for that patient) 6-12 months after enrolling in the TC PROGRAM. At least seventy percent (70%) will be from the target populations.	Develop the material and human resources needed to implement the TAKE CHARGE PROGRAM.				
	1. Develop written materials including a description of the TC PROGRAM, contract, consent form, data collection form and program protocol. Revise as necessary.	2Q		4Q	
	2. Interview all active BPM Specialists to determine interest and readiness.	1Q			
	3. Recruit additional volunteers as necessary to total at least 10 BPM Specialists in each fiscal year.	1Q		3Q	
	4. Provide, with the assistance of the Professional Education Task Force, a minimum per year of one (1) comprehensive training session and one (1) review/recertification session.	2Q	2Q	2Q	
		4Q	4Q	4Q	

State of California—Health and Welfare Agency
CONTRACT NO. _____

Department of Health Services
EXHIBIT
Page __3__ of __11__

PROJECT WORKPLAN

(Agency Name)   <u>Inland Counties Health Systems Agency</u>
(Project Title)   <u>Inland Counties Hypertension Control Program</u>
(Project Period)   To _____

The Contractor shall work toward achieving the project goals by accomplishing the following outcome objectives and activities. This shall be done by performing the specified activities and evaluating the results using the methods identified on "Project Workplan – Evaluation Plan" Form.

GOAL STATEMENT:

MEASURABLE OUTCOME OBJECTIVES	IMPLEMENTATION ACTIVITIES	ACTIVITIES TIME LINE FISCAL YEARS		
		FY 1987/88	FY 1988/89	FY 1989/90
At the end of three years TC PROGRAMS will be carried out for at least one year at a minimum of 12 church and four (4) community sites (public and private sector) located primarily in or near the cities of San Bernardino, Redlands and Riverside and in the Coachella Valley of Riverside County. At the end of the third year, BP screening and tracking will have become part of an ongoing, independent program at a minimum of eight (8) sites.	**ACTIVITY B:** Develop church and community sites for the TAKE CHARGE PROGRAM.			
	1. Develop criteria to determine the choice of screening sites. Revise as necessary.	1Q 2Q		4Q
	2. Establish at least six (6) church and two (2) community sites in FY1 and FY2, recruiting new sites as needed in FY3.	1Q		4Q
	3. Develop in the third quarter FY1, materials and protocols for institutionalizing screening and tracking programs. Revise as necessary.	3Q	1Q	4Q
	4. Review in the fourth quarter of each FY, sites with independent (institutionalized) programs to determine adherence to protocol, viability.	4Q	4Q	4Q

FIGURE 8.9. *Sample Timeline for Hypertension Control Program*

SOURCE: Pages reset from an actual Project Workplan of the Inland Counties Health System Agency, Riverside, California, 1987. Used with permission.

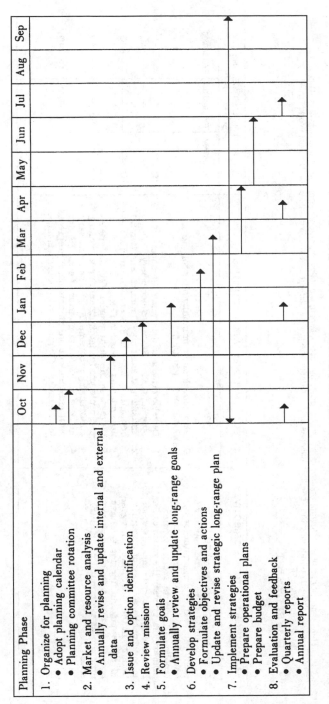

FIGURE 8.10. *Sample Timeline for Strategic Planning Hospital Operation*

SOURCE: Peters, J. P. *A Strategic Planning Process for Hospitals.* Chicago: American Hospital Publishing, 1985. Used with permission.

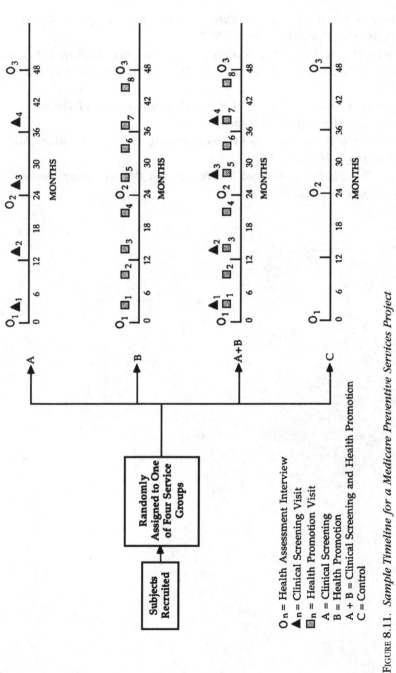

FIGURE 8.11. *Sample Timeline for a Medicare Preventive Services Project*

SOURCE: From "Implementing Medicare Preventative Health Services Demonstrations for the Elderly," J. P. Morrissey, A. M. Jackman, and J. K. Norburn of the Dept. of Social Medicine and the Center for Heath Services Research, University of North Carolina at Chapel Hill (Conference report). Used with permission.

References

1. Bloch, A. *Murphy's Law and Other Reasons Why Things Go Wrong.* Los Angeles: Price/Stern/Sloan, 1977.

2. Digan, M. B. and Carr, P. A. *Introduction to Program Planning: A Basic Text for Community Health Education.* Philadelphia: Lea & Febiger, 1981.

3. Spiegel, A. D. and Hyman, H. H. *Basic Health Planning Methods.* Rockville, MD: Aspen Publishing, 1978.

4. Brickner, W. H. and Cope, D. M. *The Planning Process.* Cambridge, MA: Winthrop Publishers, 1977.

5. Nutt, P. C. *Planning Methods for Health and Related Organizations.* New York: Wiley, 1984.

Chapter 9

Implementation of Programs, Services, and Projects: Putting the Plan into Action

THE PAROUZZI PRINCIPLE

Given a bad start, trouble will increase at an exponential rate.[1]

FIRST LAW OF CORPORATE PLANNING

Anything that can be changed will be changed until there is no time left to change anything.[1]

LAW OF REVELATION

The hidden flaw never remains hidden.[2]

CHAPTER OBJECTIVES

The main purposes of this chapter are to:

1. Define and explain implementation.

2. Understand how to go about the implementation process and the importance of an implementation plan.

3. Explain the final preparation concerns by addressing the Who, What, Why, When, Where, and How questions.

4. Review basic start-up issues such as marketing, community education, and open houses.

5. Present general activities to be done when starting a project.

6. Present barriers to implementation.

7. Describe how to open a new project and manage work flow in the first phases.

8. Present planning questions for implementation.

STEP 9

Implementation of the Project

- Make final preparations, and plan marketing, community education, an open house, and so on.

- Be sure all equipment, services, utilities, licenses, and permits are in place.

- Open the project or service.

Implementation Defined

Terms that are synonyms with implementation are *fulfill, perform, execute. Implementation* is the process of putting a project, service, or program into effect—to fulfill the planning process and accomplish the setting up and management of the execution of a project. Once Steps 1 through 8 of the Planning Model are complete, it is time to execute the plan. The *fulfilling* the planning process is when administration steps forward and puts the plan into full effect. When monies are allocated, authorization is given, and all other administrative sanctions are in place, the implementation step begins. In simple terms, the planner is ready to utilize the resources, materials, and methods to do what has been planned. It is time to take care of *needs* as determined by the needs assessment.

Implementation Plan

When this step begins, a separate plan for implementation is required for all projects. The implementation plan is unique for each project. A community health education project will have a certain set of activities and a plan for its implementation; this plan would be different from what would be necessary to a health insurance counseling program for the elderly.

An implementation plan is the process by which an organization lays out the recommendations to accomplish the project. Plan implementation utilizes a combination of methods including advocacy and financial and technical assistance.[3]

Implementation is the most critical part of the planning process; a plan that is not implemented is no plan at all. Even though implementation is the next step toward the end of the planning model, administrators of the organization should start to think about implementation at the initial discussion of the plan. When administration approves a plan, they also should plan to implement it. (See Table 9.1.) The planner has to assume that an approval to plan is an approval to implement. Why waste time and effort developing a plan for implementation that cannot be put into action to achieve the desired outcome? It would be best to delay implementation if the project cannot be effectively put into action.

Organizational Change and Project Implementation

It seems fundamental to human nature to dislike change. Change is a disruption of the routine and can cause stress. Thus, organizational change and its effect on those affected by the implementation of a new project should be considered. Information and communication are factors that reduce the impact of stress due to change. Administration and planning must communicate, and make clear to those involved, how the implementation process should be accomplished, what is expected of each individual, and how the change is to take place. Efficient and effective communication with all employee levels reduces stress, elicits support, and reduces the negative effects of change caused by project implementation.[4]

TABLE 9.1. *Developing an Implementation Plan*

1. Clearly state and assign tasks and activities; who does what for whom.
2. Assign someone to be totally responsible for each activity and be sure that this person coordinates with all persons who are to carry out each different task.
3. Clearly set forth all preparatory steps prior to doing each activity. (Refer to Figure 9.1.)
4. List steps in the order in which they must occur. This is similar to timeline development.
5. Check dates, time frames, and timelines to ensure that an adequate amount of time has been allowed for each phase, activity, and step.
6. Determine when and how each step should begin and end.
7. Use evaluation processes and timelines effectively to ensure a quality program is being implemented.
8. Consult with or coordinate with any organizations affected by the implementation of the new project or any activity of the implementation process.
9. Specify what resources, equipment, and materials will be needed and the source of each.
10. Specify what constraints or barriers need to be addressed.
11. Ascertain that all people involved clearly understand what is expected of them and that they understand the timelines.
12. Set up a reporting system so each manager responsible for certain phases or activities can communicate the progress, needs, and problems he or she cannot solve back to the administrator.

SOURCE: Adapted from National Heart, Lung and Blood Institute's *Handbook for Improving High Blood Pressure Control in the Community.*

Developing the Implementation Strategy

> *I keep six honest serving-men*
> *(they taught me all I know);*
> *Their names are*
> *WHAT and WHY and WHEN and*
> *HOW and WHERE and WHO.*
> *I send them over land and sea,*
> *I sent them east and west;*
> *But after they have worked for me,*
> *I give them all a rest.*

From "The Elephant's Child"
by J. Rudyard Kipling

For project implementation to go smoothly, it is important to determine and assign appropriate personnel to appropriate tasks.

PLANNING QUESTIONS

☐ Who is to do what tasks?

☐ What tasks and activities need to be done?

☐ When should certain tasks be started or completed and by whom?

☐ Have responsibilities been assigned to the appropriate persons?

☐ How are the activities and tasks to be accomplished?

☐ Why are the activities being done, and are they necessary?

☐ Who does what for whom?

☐ In what order are the activities to be done and when?

☐ What resources are to be used and when?

An implementation plan assumes that for every activity there is a reaction. If resources, materials, and personnel are put into the project, there should be some outcome. The friends of J. Rudyard Kipling have gained widespread use in planning. A widely accepted list, containing nine factors, is used to plan implementation activities. The factors are:

- *Why*—the effect of the objectives to be achieved.
- *What*—the activities required to achieve the objectives.
- *Who*—the individuals responsible for each activity.
- *When*—a chronological sequence of activities and timing in relation to project implementation activities or organization events.
- *How*—the materials, supplies, technology, devices, methods, media, approaches, flow of activities (patients), or techniques to be used.
- *Where*—which activities will take place at what location—in the community, at the health promotion site, facility, office, clinic, center?
- *Cost*—an estimate of expenses for materials, personnel, facilities, and time.
- *Feedback*—when and how to tell if the activities are happening as they should be and if adjustments are needed; use timelines.[5]

- *Evaluation*—the assessment of progress, success, efficiency, effectiveness, quality, use of resources, meeting goals and objectives, effect on target population, short-term results, long-term outcomes.

Implementation Worksheets

Successful implementation of a project or program can be more assured if checklists and worksheets listing things to do are used by planners and administration. The planner and administration need to have clear paths to follow and clear lists of activities to execute. The more the planner can spell out what needs to be done and when likely success will be realized, the fewer the problems will be. Failing to use planning tools, such as worksheets and checklists, will almost guarantee problems—short-sighted decisions, wrong decisions, wasted resources, and unnecessary delays.

The *Planning Wheel* is one form of checklist that has been used in planning (see Figure 9.1). The value of the Planning Wheel is that it breaks the project down into workable units, like cutting a pie into pieces; it is a first step in organizing work and activities in logical units that are similar. The Planning Wheel is more general in use, lacking detail and specifics. There is no list of actual activities to be executed. Therefore, further effort needs to be put into creating checklists with activities to be developed. Activity worksheets are useful tools to meet this need. (See Figure 9.2.)

A worksheet can be developed, prepared, and managed for each major activity or phase of the implementation of the project. If a project has five phases, five different worksheets would be prepared for the overall implementation. If a different manager is assigned to each phase, the manager or responsible person also should be written at the top of the worksheet. Each responsible person needs to develop his or her own checklists and worksheets as well.

Manpower Planning

For a program to be successful, it has to have good people. Thus, the selection and/or hiring of well-qualified personnel should be included in the initial phase of implementation. It is always easier to choose a person who is familiar to the administration to head up a project

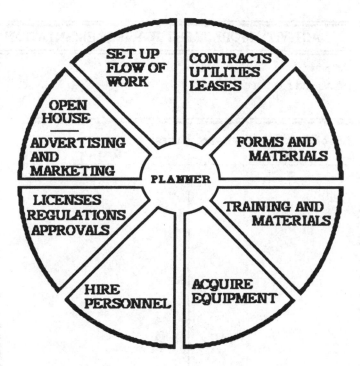

FIGURE 9.1. *Planning Wheel—Implementation Checklist*

instead of hiring another more qualified person. If the project is one on health education, qualified and formally prepared health educators should be hired. It may be handy to put a social worker or nurse in a health education position, but this is not going to guarantee quality training or success. Clinical areas are protected by licensing laws but such protection is lacking for nonlicensed personnel such as health educators or health administrators. In clinical areas, for example, only properly qualified personnel should fill the positions. This concept is also true for all other areas—properly qualified personnel should fill the positions.

How many people are needed to implement a project? Because some accreditation requirements apply in clinical areas, guidelines often set staffing levels and they should be followed. Realistic manpower determination needs to be exercised in uncontrolled areas. Hiring too many persons is a waste of resources; they actually can get in the way, but too few can ensure failure of the project. So, personnel needs have to be realistically and effectively determined. A manpower planning worksheet can assist in this process (see Figure 9.3). The use

ACTIVITY WORKSHEET FOR IMPLEMENTATION		
Activity: Focus and Key Issues:		

List of Specific Activities and Duties:

	WHO	WHAT	WHEN
1.			
2.			
3.			
4.			
5.			
6.			
7.			
8.			
9.			
10.			
11.			
12.			
13.			
14.			
15.			

FIGURE 9.2. *Sample of Activity Worksheet for Project Implementation*

MANPOWER PLANNING WORKSHEET			
ACTIVITY: List specific activities, personnel needed, numbers of personnel required and when (by what date).			
ACTIVITY	PERSONNEL TYPE	NUMBER	DATE
1.			
2.			
3.			
4.			
5.			
6.			
7.			
8.			
9.			
10.			
11.			
12.			
13.			
14.			
15.			

FIGURE 9.3. *Sample Manpower Planning Worksheet*

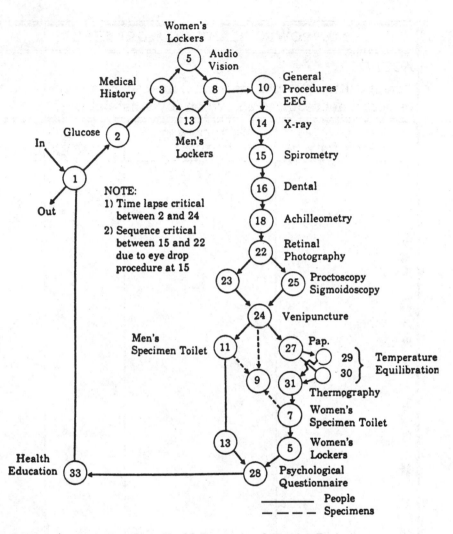

FIGURE 9.4. *Work Flow for a Health Promotion Screening Project*

SOURCE: From *Guidelines for Functional Programming, Equipping and Designing Hospital Outpatient and Emergency Activities.* Washington, DC: Health Resources Administration of the U.S. Department of Health, Education and Welfare, 1977.

of the flow charting techniques as shown in Figure 9.4 can assist some projects in determining manpower needs.

The Federal Health Resources and Services Administration has established a set of steps to assess a community and eliminate disparities in the community which is called the *Community Progress Scale*. The scale has ten steps which are presented below.

Step	Description
1. Catalyst steps are developed to *ready* the community and to move forward.	A catalyst emerges with community groups ready to convene.
2. Community dialogue occurs with community groups talking.	The community groups talk about how to increase access and reduce disparities.
3. The community champions commitment.	The community publicly commits to the vision of 100% access and zero health disparities.
4. The community declares the result they desire.	The community declares the access they want to create and the disparities they want to eliminate.
5. Community leadership group aligns community assets.	Community players align existing resources to increase access and/or reduce disparities.
6. Primary care system is built in the community.	The community builds the health-care delivery system that it needs.
7. Results are seen in eliminating disparities and developing the community.	The community produces results with access increased and disparities reduced.
8. Public celebration and open house is conducted. News conferences are called for newspaper and television.	Accomplishments are publicly presented and celebrated.
9. A program for continuous quality improvement is developed.	The community assesses its continual progress and continues to improve community health.
10. Goal is achieved and is used to benchmark against.	Community declares victory on increasing access and the reduction in disparities. Benchmarks are established.

Barriers to Implementation

Planning is the easiest part of program development. It is relatively simple to speculate and visualize programs in place and operating smoothly. In reality, program development does not always go so easily. Administration and potential recipients of the service are enthusiastic until it comes time to commit time, energy, space, money, personnel, and resources to bring the program into existence. Therefore, a major barrier to implementation of any project is the commitment of administration.

TABLE 9.2. *Some Possible Barriers to Implementation*

- Lack of interest by the potential participants that may be due to a poor need assessment or lack of one, because need assessments should identify this problem.
- Lack of understanding by administration, participants, staff, board, or community organizations, often due to poor communication.
- Lack of financial payment system, reimbursement, or support.
- Lack of quality services.
- Inadequate quantity of services.
- Lack of access to services.
- Insufficient communication about the existence of the service; little or no marketing or poor marketing.
- Unacceptable service or dissatisfaction with the service.
- Placing personnel in positions for which they are not trained or qualified.
- Poor management of the implementation and initial phases of the project.
- Lack of adjustment to changes occurring in the planning and implementation.
- Limited access to transportation or none is available.
- Legal and regulatory matters not correctly attended to.
- Cultural, ethnic, and racial issues not considered or accounted for.
- Lack of the development of effective policy and procedures.
- Improper or inadequate manpower, equipment, facilities, and the like.
- Failure to effectively and efficiently use known planning techniques.
- Hiring or selecting unqualified, improperly trained or educated personnel for nonlicensed areas, i.e., health education, health administration, social services, and so on.

Each project has its own set of limitations, impediments, and barriers to implementation (see Table 9.2). Thus, to present a list of all possible barriers to a specific plan, a planner might encounter an almost impossible chore. The barriers to implementing a health education program for the elderly would be much different from the barriers to implementing a hospital outpatient clinic for the elderly. However, a general position of resistance can be generalized across most projects. If administration likes a project, sees value in it, and will support it, implementation and success are more likely to occur—success can be better assured.

Administrators can subtly fail to fully support a project. That is, some administrators verbally and publicly support a project but quietly to themselves, or among certain members of the staff, express doubt about the project. Yet, the administrator moves ahead as if it is supported. This approach programs the project for failure. The administrators must do whatever they can to ensure they are not programming the plan for failure. It is best for the administrators to be honest with themselves and openly admit their lack of support. If an above-board approach is used, much frustration and loss of time, money, and precious resources will not be wasted. Planners would rather not waste time and resources on a project that is not fully supported.

Work Flow Planning

Planning the work flow is highly critical for some types of projects and not so critical for others. "Community Health Education for the Elderly" as a program does not require a great deal of work flow planning. On the other hand, outpatient clinics or other ambulatory clinic-type programs that require several stations be visited and several activities or procedures be conducted during a single visit will require work flow planning (see Figure 9.4). In health promotion screening, initial intakes have to be conducted, several different testing procedures have to be carried out, records need to be created, tests reported, and so on. The flow of work for each separate screening site has to be determined as does the work flow for the overall project. Complex work flow may be faced if screenings are to be conducted at several sites on either a sequential or regularly scheduled basis (see Figure 9.5).

One of the best methods for planning work flow is to use flow charting techniques. Flow charting is useful because it helps the planner put the flow of activities, work, and patients into picture form. Also, it graphically shows personnel needs. The methods and approaches to flow charting have many common characteristics and they have a beginning point at which the individual enters the system. Arrows or lines are used to show the flow of the patient through the system. Boxes or circles are used to show events. When one event has been completed, the work flow moves on to the next. Flow charting helps the planner thoroughly think through each and every activity, decide what is done first and what has to be done next, and so on. Flow charting of work flow also assists in manpower planning. From the flow chart, workstations are determined, which also shows the number of workers needed.

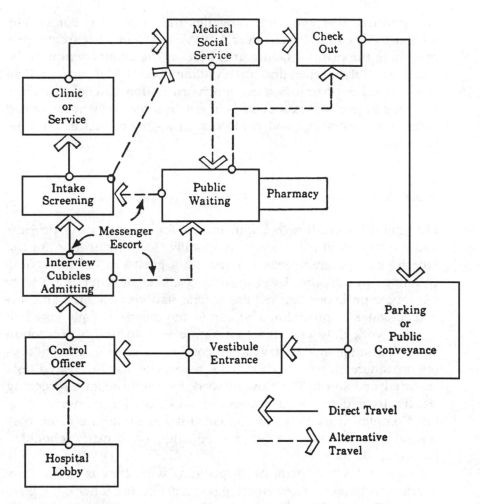

FIGURE 9.5. *Work Flow for Planning Development of an Outpatient Clinic*

SOURCE: From *Guidelines for Functional Programming, Equipping and Designing Hospital Outpatient and Emergency Activities.* Washington, DC: Health Resources Administration of the U.S. Department of Health, Education and Welfare, 1977.

Anticipating Problems

In the implementation process, the astute and effective planner must anticipate the possibility of things going wrong and needs to consider all potential things that could go wrong, especially those that will cause serious damage if not dealt with quickly. If problems are anticipated, they can be resolved more easily should they occur in the implementation process. Any deviation from an expected outcome or from the plan will need to be managed, remedied, and the project put back on course. This is referred to as *contingency planning.*[7] The loss of a key planner or administrator; a fire in the new building; unanticipated government regulations; financial changes in the organization; new technology; unavailability of materials, equipment, or personnel; and so on—all need to be a part of a contingency plan. The foundation for contingency planning is the "What if . . . ?" questions:

- What if we cannot find a technician to run the new high-tech equipment?
- What if we cannot find personnel in shortage areas such as a physical therapist for our new clinic?
- What if the price of the new equipment goes up before we can purchase it?
- What if hardly any senior citizens show up for our health screening program?

The planner needs to anticipate both the extent, or degree of criticality, of a problem and the probability of it occurring. An event with a low probability of occurring, though it is a critical event, must be solved and the issues closely addressed up front. For example, a certain piece of equipment may be needed to do a specialized screening procedure, but the equipment is in great demand and hard to acquire. Without the equipment, the project cannot proceed. It is critical that an all-out effort be made to ensure that the equipment is available when needed. Contingency plans need to focus on a critical issue or even that may have an impact on the implementation of the project.[7]

A second part of contingency planning is to develop plans and tactics to deal with possible occurrences in each step or phase of the implementation process. The aim is to neutralize or offset the negative impact of any event if and when it occurs. Alternative contingencies or tactics should be identified. The organization's ability, or constraints, to deal with the problem need to be considered. Through asking the "What if . . . ?" questions, problems can be anticipated and decisions can be made in advance so actions to take or tactics to deal with any event can be in place when or if it occurs. Decisions about what to do and tactics should be as specific as possible.[7] Expected outcomes can be calculated and accounted for with greater success and less problems will be encountered.[7]

PLANNING QUESTIONS

☐ Has an implementation plan been developed?

☐ Has administration and the planners considered how the organizational change will impact the organization and the personnel involved?

☐ Has the planner considered the Who, Why, When, What, How, and Where issues of the implementation process?

☐ Have the planner and administrators used the planning worksheets and other useful planning techniques and approaches?

☐ Have barriers and impediments to implementation been considered and dealt with?

☐ Have manpower planning issues been considered and resolved?

☐ Has work flow been considered and managed?

☐ Have problems been anticipated and has contingency planning been conducted?

References

1. Bloch, A. *Murphy's Law, Book Three.* Los Angeles: Price/Stern/Sloan, 1982.
2. Bloch, A. *Murphy's Law, Book Two.* Los Angeles: Price/Stern/Sloan, 1981.
3. Timmreck, T. C. *Dictionary of Health Services Management.* Owings Mills, MD: National Health Publishing, 1987.
4. Rowe, A. J., Mason, R. O., Dickel, K. E., and Snyder, N. H. *Strategic Management,* 3d ed. Reading, MA: Addison-Wesley, 1989.
5. Spiegel, A. D. and Hyman, H. H. *Basic Health Planning Methods.* Rockville, MD: Aspen Publishing, 1978.
6. National Heart, Lung and Blood Institute. *Handbook for Improving High Blood Pressure Control in the Community.* Washington, DC: U.S. Government Printing Office, 1977.
7. Steiner, G. A. *Strategic Planning: What Every Manager Must Know—A Step-by-Step Guide.* New York: Free Press, 1979.

Chapter 10

Evaluation and Feedback

BIONDI'S LAW

If your project doesn't work, look for the part you didn't think was important.[1]

DRAZEN'S LAW OF RESTITUTION

The time it takes to rectify a situation is inversely proportional to the time it took to do the damage.[2]

CHAPTER OBJECTIVES

The main purposes of this chapter are to:

1. Define and explain evaluation and feedback.

2. Understand how to conduct the evaluation process and the importance of evaluation and feedback.

3. Explain evaluation and assessment approaches and methods.

4. Review basic evaluation issues.

5. Present barriers to evaluation.

6. Present planning questions for evaluation.

STEP 10
Evaluation and Feedback

- Are the objectives being met?

- Are the activities effective and efficient?

- Are timelines being met?

- Is there a regular formal evaluation system in place, and is it used seriously?

- Conduct impact evaluation and outcome evaluation.

Definitions

Evaluation has a broad meaning and is often defined according to the setting in which it is used. For the purpose of program development and planning, *evaluation* is defined as the process of determining the degree to which an objective of a program or procedure has been completed or met. It usually includes a review of the objectives, and establishing the criteria used to measure the degree of success.[3] Evaluation more generally includes the process of comparing an object of interest with an acceptable standard, as well as concern for effectiveness, efficiency and quality of activities, and performance.

Evaluation is complex and diverse in both concept and function. The setting in which evaluation is to occur, the type of service or program to be evaluated, and extent and level of evaluation, as well as a whole range of management functions and requirements influencing the role and approach of evaluation, dictate how and what is to be evaluated. For example, evaluation in health promotion can be used to measure health activation, behavioral change, gains made, participation by workers, change in risk factors—all evaluating the participant. Programmatic activities and participation are the objectives being measured. Cost-effectiveness, cost-benefit analysis, days of work lost (or gained), effectiveness, efficiency, accountability, manpower, workloads, marketing results, goals and objectives being obtained, effective implementation, organization, communication, control, and other management factors are evaluated from an administrative position. Health promotion outcomes desired by management of a company may not be the ones the health promotion planner wants. Companies are reluctant to give up the bottom line for expensive facilities, equipment, time spent away from the job, and so on, which may be desired or even demanded for the health promotion program.

Feedback is the positive or negative response to a system's outcomes for the purpose of influencing the planning or implementation process to produce a better outcome. Feedback occurs in the form of information being directed back to the beginning or to selected parts of a process, project, or program, with the aim of improving on it and, providing an assessment and evaluation, which in turn assists in improving quality, control, or outcomes.[3]

Both evaluation and feedback are necessary in order to steer the planning, implementation, and ongoing management of a project in the direction of its goals and objectives. The underlying aim of evaluation and feedback is to ensure efficient, effective, and quality outcomes. A successful project that has ongoing possibilities for improvement must regularly ascertain if it is on the right track and make sure the needed improvements are put in place when it is not.

Evaluation

Evaluation is a complex process that has to be actively implemented and effectively put into action at all levels and phases of a project or service. Ongoing and regular evaluation of a program should be conducted. The most useful approach to evaluation is through the development of goals, general objectives, and specific objectives. Goals and objectives are looked at to determine if they have been met, if outcomes are realized, to what extent they have been met, and what still needs to be done. Step 2 of the Model establishes the importance of an evaluation process. Step 3 and Step 6 present the need for goals and objectives and set forth how to develop and write objectives. Comparing what the objectives stated with what was supposed to be done and with what actually happened is fundamental to the evaluation process. Of the many professional fields and endeavors to use evaluation processes in recent times, health promotion has put forth the most aggressive and ambitious approach.

Evaluation in Health Promotion: Approaches and Constructs

Program development and evaluation has been the profession concept for the 1980s and 1990s for health promotion and health education. Two of the foundational constructs of evaluation, as used in health promotion and health education, that designates levels of activities are formative evaluation and summative evaluation.

Formative evaluation is a method used to assess whether a problem is occurring, the extent of the problem, and if corrective measures are needed. If a corrective measure is needed, the health promotion manager determines which intervention should be used and how successes of the corrective action are to be measured.

Summative evaluation is the second level aspect, and it has two factors to consider: program impact and program efficiency. *Program impact* is assessed by the ability of an intervention to produce its intended outcomes and to verify cause-effect relationships between intervention inputs and program outcomes. *Program efficiency* is used to ascertain if the same outcomes could have been achieved in a more effective manner at a lower cost. Cost-benefit analysis and cost-effectiveness analysis are used to measure efficiency and are at the heart of this part of the evaluation process.[5]

A related construct that has been used in evaluation is *process evaluation*. Process evaluation includes procedures, policies, work flow, materials, personnel management, performance appraisals, programmatic performance, quality, administrative effectiveness and efficiency, and other administrative inputs of the implementation process. Process evaluation as used in assessment of administration activities is often associated with summative evaluation.

Impact Outcomes Evaluation

Basic to impact outcomes is a theoretical framework through which goal outcomes are correlated with the use of resources and the cost of the program or service. Cause-effect associations are developed and studied. The *program intervention model* approach has been suggested to assist in formative evaluation efforts.

The program intervention model is based on the acronym R A S O G O:

R—Resources lead to activities

A—Activities lead to sub-objectives

S—Sub-objectives lead to objectives

O—Objectives lead to goals

G—Goals produce outcomes

O—Outcomes

The program intervention is supposed to assist in gathering data to assess the impact and effectiveness of activities that have occurred; and if those activities have met the objectives, if the objects have achieved the goals; and if outcomes are realized. What is lacking in this approach are methods of evaluation, which are up to the planner or health promotion manager to create and apply. Program type and approaches dictate the methodology of evaluation.[4]

The concept of *impact evaluation* was modified by Green and Kreuter to embrace their phases of the PRECEDE model by redefining the evaluation of program outcomes based on intermediate objectives as applied to the changes in the various phases of the model: predisposing factors, enabling factors, reinforcing factors, as well as behavioral changes and environmental changes. (Refer to PRECEDE model in Figure 5.2 on page 100.)[5]

Outcome Evaluation

Outcome evaluation in health promotion is used to assess the final results of program activities—the consequences of program management. The health promotion manager or health educator is interested in change. What are the changes seen in risk factors? What measurable changes can be identified? Have there been changes in behavior, knowledge, health activation, attitudes? Has the health status of the population been impacted with reduced morbidity and mortality? Has the health status of each individual worker or group of participants been impacted with reduced morbidity and mortality?

Impact outcome can be measured short term or long term. *Short-term impact* usually is measured by comparing intake baselines or pretest scores with assessments done at the completion of programs, for example, posttesting of health educational activities. Therefore, impact outcomes can be measured by identifying, in the clientele, improved knowledge of specific subject matter or health content areas, changes in diet, increase in exercise and fitness activities, changes in blood pressure and cholesterol levels, decreases in cigarette consumption, number of sessions attended, number of participants attending health promotion events, and so on. Short-term impact outcomes are of greatest interest to the health promotion manager or health educator and of less value to the business manager and organization.[7]

Long-term impact is an outcome measure associated with factors more difficult to connect to health promotion program activities than short-term impacts; these variables are more important to the business end of the process. Company managers are more interested in the long-term impact outcomes of health promotion than the short-term programmatic results. Long-term business impact could include: increased productivity of employees, improved morale on the job, higher levels of motivation, less absenteeism, reduced days of sick leave, reduced medical insurance premiums, reduced turnover, benefits shown to outweigh costs, and the like. If a health promotion program costs more money than the benefits the company gains, and if profitability is not improved either directly or indirectly, the company may cancel the program. In other words, if organizational and business-related benefits are not realized by the health promotion program, it will not be looked on favorably by the company or organization.[7]

The health promotion manager should actively develop data baselines and collect and analyze data, developing reports that will be of programmatic use. The wise health promotion manager sets up data-collection processes that will collect and analyze the long-term impacts/business-related factors. Business reports to the organization should be provided on a regular basis and should be couched in business-related terms common to management (not health promotion) based on the long-term impact factors.

Purposes of Evaluation

Health promotion, to be accepted in and supported by industry, business, and worksites, has to demonstrate that it can ensure that monies being put into the health promotion processes are used in the most cost-effective manner. Evaluation helps establish managerial accountability, which helps to ensure that outcomes are in line with program goals and objectives. Evaluation methods can set baselines of data to be used as reference points in analysis. Scientific knowledge can be used to justify programs, demonstrate benefits, and satisfy the business outcome expectations of organizational management. Data and baselines can demonstrate that health promotion and health education works, and that a healthier workforce equals increased productivity, reduced absences from work, decreased illness, decreased use of health care resources and profits, and improved employee morale.[5,6,7,8,9]

Evaluation Approaches and Designs

Several health promotion evaluation designs are suggested and are mentioned briefly here. For a detailed review of each of these designs, references about the specific design should be consulted.

1. *Recordkeeping/Historical Design.* Records are kept to accumulate appropriate data and charts are used to show changes that occur. Graphs and charts are used to show how well the program is progressing.
2. *Inventory Design.* Data is collected at intervals. Target dates for assessment are set and data is collected using questionnaires or other inventories. Follow-ups are also scheduled to assess long-term impact.
3. *Comparative Design.* Evaluation activities use comparison of similar or related programs. Documents or data and information are borrowed from these programs to make comparisons.
4. *Quasi-Experimental/Controlled Comparison Design.* The organization's population is compared to another similar population. Both research groups are tested using the same inventories, tests, and evaluation instruments. The participants are given the health promotion programs and the control group population is

not given anything. Data from both groups is collected within the same time period and compared.

5. *Controlled-Experimental Approach.* This approach uses random sampling. Half the worksite population participants in the health promotion activity and the other half does not. All participate in the same evaluation procedures and the data from both groups is compared.

6. *Comprehensive Research Design.* Experimental design approaches are employed with multiple groups, using random sampling and multiple evaluation measurements. Complex inferential statistical analyses are done.[9,10,11,12]

Yet there is another approach to planning and evaluation which includes several steps. The purpose of program evaluation is to gather information required to ensure that you end up with the service that is directed at the problem that it was meant to address and the service reaches the target population desired and delivers the services as intended. Although the steps are presented in the order of their occurrence, it should be noted that some of the activities can occur simultaneously. A health service problem cannot be efficiently resolved unless described with precise problem statements. These statements help to determine whether a particular problem needs the use of resources and should address: What is occurring? What should be occurring? Is there a discrepancy between these two? Is the nature and extent of the discrepancy serious enough to justify using limited resources to reduce or eliminate it?

The first step is for the planning staff to provide technical assistance to the personnel working on the project in identifying, defining, assessing and prioritizing problems and needs of the target population. The planners are to identify and describe health problems of the population to be served. To succeed at this, *Form 1* (Figure 10.1) is a helpful tool in completing this process. This form helps to identify what problems exist and what the needs are. It also provides for planning for an intervention for each need or gap in services identified. The search for health problems should be limited to the most relevant needs and, those that are bring to pass the mission and goals of the agency/organization.

The next step is to clarify the reason to conduct the evaluation study. Was the study requested by an administrative agency or was it

	PROBLEM IDENTIFICATION PHASE			NEEDS ASSESSMENT PHASE			INTERVENTION PLANNING PHASE
EXPECTED: What are the desired health services?	OBSERVED: What are the actual health services that are in place?	PROBLEMS: Articulate gaps between what is desired and the actual state of affairs.	CAUSES: What are the primary and secondary determinants of the problem?	REQUIRED: What is required to alleviate determinants or problems?	AVAILABLE: What services are available to alleviate determinants or problems?	NEEDS: Articulate gaps between what is required to alleviate determinants and what is available.	PROGRAM: What program activities will meet identified needs and alleviate the determinants and solve the problem?

FIGURE 10.1. *Form 1*

initiated by a grant proposal? Is the evaluation to be made to justify an already-made decision or to terminate a program? Is the evaluation conducted to gain information so decisions can be made about the worth of developing a program or service?

Identify the stakeholders. A stakeholder is anyone who has a vested interest in the program or service to be developed: anyone who might be affected by or interested in the outcomes of the evaluation. It is important to identify stakeholders at onset of the evaluation initiative. If certain stakeholders are ignored they can sabotage the initiative. A committee of all of the stakeholders could be formed to ensure their input.

A recommended approach to identifying health problems is to determine the discrepancies between what is expected (illness rates), utilizing the opinions of health experts and past experiences, and what is observed based on the morbidity rates and data relating to the identified health problem. The greater the variance between the data and rates, the greater the problem and the greater the need for addressing the problem. This is also useful in setting program priorities.

Once health problems are identified they should be described in a great deal of detail so as to understand the extent of the problem and the nature of the issues surrounding the problem. To describe the health problem ones needs to collect information about the time, place (environment), and person, epidemiologically speaking. Questions need to be asked, such as: Who is affected by the problem (elderly, children, females, males)? How susceptible are they? How severe is the problem? How prevalent is the problem? Where do those affected by the problem reside, work, attend school, or receive health care? When and where did the problem originate?, and Are there secular (long-term) trends, cyclical or seasonal variations, or short-term changes in the problems? From this information one can determine who is affected and who may require assistance in overcoming the health problem, behavior, or condition, how common the health problem is, how serious the problem is, where those affected live and/or work, and how long the problem has persisted.

The next step is to prioritize the health problems. Health planners and health services administrators must carefully weigh their options and determine where limited resources can most efficiently and effectively be applied. Prioritizing requires objective criteria for systematically determining which problems are most important.

Some considerations include determining whether the planning or organization has the authority to act; the extent of the problems and the seriousness of the health problem; the state of the knowledge available to address the problem; availability of human and technical resources required; desires of community leaders to intervene; the public outcry demanding an intervention; and the final consideration and the costs necessary to intervene.

The next step is to identify the determinants of the health problem chosen for the intervention. One way determinants can be identified is by conducting studies. The Strategy Planning Guide (SPG) can be useful. An SPG can be completed for each health problem selected. The planner next decides which health problem determinants need to be addressed.

Next the planner assesses the needs or gaps to address the health problem determinants (such as smoking causing low-birth-weight babies) in order to remove the problem. To be able to identify needs a need assessment has to be completed. Need assessments were addressed earlier in this book in Chapter 5.

After the need assessment is completed, the planner needs to determine the internal and external fiscal, material, and human resources available to meet the needs that were identified and to evaluate the interventions.

The planner next formulates objectives in order to address the health problem at hand. Objectives should be measurable, have benchmarks to judge the results against, have a set time period to be completed in, and be realistic and reasonable. Then each objective should have a strategy develop to help reach the objective. Strategies are detailed statements of what should be done to reach each objective. Rationale should be developed to justify each strategy and should address why a particular strategy can be effective in meeting the objective and solving the need. Tactics need to be developed to meet the strategies. Tactics are the specific actions needed to complete the strategies, i.e., which activities and approaches will work best to meet the strategies. Once strategies and tactics are selected, they need to be communicated to the evaluation staff. Conduct a preevaluation appraisal to determine the evaluation parameters.

An evaluation plan should be formulated. It should set forth how the evaluation is to be carried out and describe the proposed evaluation process. The plan can use goals and objectives to measure progress toward completion.

The evaluation plan should provide:

- Necessary background information on each strategy/tactic
- Questions to be answered by the project
- Theoretical assumptions tested
- Findings compared with the program goals and objectives
- Information about the sources of data on each evaluation question, objective, etc.
- The qualitative and quantitative data-gathering methods used to collect information
- The forms or instruments to gather data
- A diagram that sets forth the data-gathering study design
- How to code, enter, and manage the collected data needs to be determined
- Explanations of how qualitative and quantitative data will be analyzed
- Data summarized in tables and charts and graphs developed
- A timeline should be developed specifying when tasks will be carried out and completed
- A list of personnel needed to complete each task
- A budget that itemizes all required resources
- Complete, final written report

Quantitative Approaches

A multitude of quantitative approaches for use in evaluation are available. Surveys, questionnaires, and various tests can be given to participants, staff, and the community to determine effectiveness of many of the evaluation criteria presented here. The results can be tabulated and analyzed by statistics, and organized into reports or formal presentations to be given to management. Pretests can be compared to posttests and results can be shown in graphic and table form, all of which provide a highly accurate and sophisticated approach to the evaluation process. The limitation of this approach often is the lack of expertise and the cost of producing reports of the results. Planners should consider how quantitative they wish the evaluation process to become; how quantitative does administration want it to be? The planner will then structure the evaluation process accordingly.

Reasons for and Uses of Evaluation

The main reason a planner conducts evaluations is to assess accomplishments and identify problems or limitations. Evaluation is a process that is not always welcomed with open arms. It has been used to develop justifications to force departments in an organization to carry out certain activities. It also can take up a lot of time, which some managers feel might be better used for work-related tasks.

Many reasons for evaluation exist; the following are some possibilities:

- To find out if the program or service is carrying out the mission of the organization.
- To ascertain if overall goals and objectives are being met.
- To determine if the programs or services are deviating from the direction they should be going.
- To see if the subcomponents of the project—i.e., costs, budgets, personnel, equipment, work flow, supplies, and so on—are staying in line.
- To determine if priorities are set correctly and meet the needs of the project and organization.
- To ascertain if the timeline projections are on time.
- To find out if each phase or if each specific aspect of the program is being as successful as it can be.
- To indicate where intervention is needed, or where program direction needs correction.
- To ascertain if work flow snags are impeding the effectiveness of the service.

The major use of evaluation is to assess the outcomes that occurred as a result of the implementation of the program or service.

Variables in Assessment and Evaluation

In health and human services, several standard variables are used to evaluate the effectiveness and efficiency of any service or program. Table 10.1 lists variables the planner should consider to determine if a program is working and how well it is working.

TABLE 10.1. *Variables to Determine Program Effectiveness and Efficiency*

Availability

- Can the clients or patients get to the service or program when they need it or desire to receive it?
- Geographically, are enough (quantity) services being offered for those who want to attend or participate?

Accessibility

- Can the client or patient use the service or program that is offered?
- Is the cost reasonable and can the participant get transportation to the service?
- Are there barriers to getting to the service?

Quantity

- Are the services or programs being offered often enough and in enough places to accommodate those who wish to participate?

Quality

- Are the services provided at the highest level that can be offered in all aspects of the service or program?

Cost

- Do the costs, charges, or insurance reimbursements allow the client or patient to access the service?
- Are the charges reasonable?

Acceptability

- Are the services or programs of the type, nature, and quality to satisfy the participants?
- Are the services offered on a regular basis and in a timely fashion?
- Is waiting time reasonable or are there long lines?
- Are appointments available without waiting a long time?
- How satisfied with the service or program are the participants?

Continuity

- Does the program have succession and ongoing services that build one on the other?
- Is the patient's or client's information passed on to those who need to know it in an expedient manner to provide overall coordinated services?

Health Promotion Evaluation Standards

Four basic health promotion evaluation standards have been suggested:

1. *Retrospective/Historical Comparison.* Outcomes of the current program or project are compared to previous programs or projects.
2. *Theoretical Comparison.* Concepts and expectations of previous research findings are used as a standard to compare current program results to.
3. *Absolute Standards Comparison.* The highest level of attainment based on theoretical standards or research findings are used to compare current program results and outcomes. The standard is an ideal and possibly is not attainable.
4. *Average or Negotiated Comparisons.* Various levels of outcomes and standards are considered and decided on as the levels to be aimed for in program attainment. An average of established or past standards are often used.[11,12,13]

PLANNING QUESTIONS

☐ What is the purpose of the evaluation and what is to be achieved?[10,11]

☐ Should the project, service, or program be continued in the same manner it has been done in the past?

☐ How can the practices and procedures be changed and improved?

☐ Which approaches, activities, or methods have the best outcomes? Which have the worst outcomes?

☐ Could this program be expanded and be successful at other sites or in other organizations?

☐ How well has the budgeting process worked?

☐ Can the results of the evaluation process be used to make the project or service better?

☐ Does the evaluation process give you the information necessary to improve, make adjustments, or increase the functioning of the service or program?

☐ What kind of change in the program is desired?

☐ How is a change to be brought about?

☐ How reliable are the measures of effectiveness and efficiency that are employed?

☐ Were there any unexpected occurrences or consequences?

☐ How effectively did the program planning, implementation, and management activities attain the goals and objectives?

☐ What desirable and undesirable side effects occurred?

CDC's Framework for Program Evaluation

The Centers for Disease Control and Prevention, through their Evaluation Working Group, have set forth an effective program evaluation process (see Figure 10.2). This is a systematic way to improve and account for public health actions that involves procedures that are useful, feasible, ethical, and accurate. The framework guides public health professionals in their use of program evaluation. It is a practical tool, designed to summarize and organize essential elements of program evaluation. The framework comprises steps in program evaluation practice and standards for effective program evaluation. Adhering to the steps and standards of this framework will allow an understanding of each program's context and will improve how program evaluations are conceived and conducted. When potential decisions or program changes are needed, employing evaluation procedures that are explicit, formal, and justifiable becomes important. Understanding the logic, reasoning, and values of evaluation that are reflected in this framework can lead to lasting impacts, such as basing decisions on systematic judgments instead of unfounded assumptions.

Purposes

The framework was developed to summarize and organize the essential elements of program evaluation; provide a common frame of reference

FIGURE 10.2. *CDC Evaluation Wheel*

for conducting evaluations; clarify the steps in program evaluation; review standards for effective program evaluation; and address misconceptions about the purposes and methods of program evaluation.

Scope

Throughout this report, the term "program" is used to describe the object of evaluation; it applies to any organized public health action. This definition is deliberately broad because the framework can be applied to almost any public health activity, including:

- Direct service interventions
- Community mobilization efforts
- Research initiatives
- Surveillance systems
- Policy development activities

- Outbreak investigations
- Laboratory diagnostics
- Communication campaigns
- Infrastructure building projects
- Training and education services
- Administrative systems, and others

Steps and Standards

The following summarizes the steps in program evaluation practice with the most important subpoints for each, as well as the standards that govern effective program evaluation.

Steps in Evaluation Practice

Engage stakeholders: Those involved, those affected, primary intended users.

Describe the program: Need, expected effects, activities, resources, stage, context, logic model.

Focus the evaluation design: Purpose, users, uses, questions, methods, agreements.

Gather credible evidence: Indicators, sources, quality, quantity, logistics.

Justify conclusions: Standards, analysis/synthesis, interpretation, judgment, recommendations.

Ensure use and share lessons learned: Design, preparation, feedback, follow-up, dissemination.

Standards for "Effective" Evaluation

Utility: Serve the information needs of intended users.

Feasibility: Be realistic, prudent, diplomatic, and frugal.

Propriety: Behave legally, ethically, and with due regard for the welfare of those involved and those affected.

Accuracy: Reveal and convey technically accurate information

(The steps and standards are used together throughout the evaluation process. For each step there is a subset of standards that are generally most relevant to consider.)

Applying the Framework

Conducting Optimal Evaluations   Public health professionals can no longer question whether to evaluate their programs; instead, the appropriate questions are: What is the best way to evaluate? What are we learning from evaluation? How will we use the learning to make public health efforts more effective? The framework for program evaluation helps answer these questions by guiding its users in selecting evaluation strategies that are useful, feasible, ethical, and accurate. To use the recommended framework in a specific program context requires skill in both the science and art of program evaluation. The challenge is to devise an optimal—as opposed to an ideal— strategy. An optimal strategy is one that accomplishes each step in the framework in a way that accommodates the program context and meets or exceeds all relevant standards.

Assembling an Evaluation Team   Harnessing and focusing the efforts of a collaborative group is one approach to conducting an optimal evaluation. A team approach can succeed when small groups of carefully selected persons decide what the evaluation must accomplish, and they pool resources to implement the plan. A leader must be designated to coordinate the team and maintain continuity throughout the process. In addition, those with group facilitation skills might be asked to help elicit unspoken expectations regarding the program and to expose hidden values that partners bring to the effort. Decision makers and others who guide program direction can help focus the evaluation design on questions that address specific users and uses. They can also set logistic parameters for the evaluation's scope, time line, and deliverables. All organizations, even those that are able to find evaluation team members within their own agency, should collaborate with partners and take advantage of community resources when assembling an evaluation team. This strategy increases the available resources and enhances the evaluation's credibility. Furthermore, a diverse team of engaged stakeholders has a greater probability of conducting a culturally competent evaluation.

Addressing Common Concerns   The expense of an evaluation is relative; the cost depends on the questions being asked and the level of certainty desired for the answers (i.e., sending out surveyors). The framework encourages conducting evaluations that are timed strategically to provide necessary feedback. This makes integrating evaluation with program practice possible. Although circumstances exist where controlled environments and elaborate analytic techniques are needed, most public health program evaluations do not require such methods. Instead, the practical approach endorsed by this framework focuses on questions that will improve the program by using context-sensitive methods and analytic techniques that summarize accurately the meaning of qualitative and quantitative information. The framework encourages an evaluation approach that is designed to be helpful and engages all interested stakeholders in a process that welcomes their participation.

Steps in and Levels of Evaluation

Steps in Evaluation

Many approaches to the evaluation process have been attempted but no one right way has been established. Several lists have been set forth for the evaluation process; one method involves a four-step process[12]:

Step 1. Set goals and objectives. Operationalize the process with detailed criteria that are set forth and used.

Step 2. Collection of data. Establish a system and procedure to collect the evaluation data and analyze it.

Step 3. Analysis of the evaluation data. Quantitative analysis through statistics, descriptions, and inferences. Qualitative analysis through reports, verbal descriptions, logs, interviews, and client reports.

Step 4. Adjust, modify, and change the program. Improve the service or program as a result of the findings of the data and its analysis.

Another approach has six steps to the evaluation process[8]:

1. Review and identification of the goals and objective to be evaluated.

2. Complete an analysis of the problems that the project or program faces.

3. Provide a clear and precise description and standardization of the program or service.

4. Provide a measure of the amount of change that is needed in the program or service.

5. Determine whether the problems or changes are due to matters within the organization or from an external cause.

6. What are the lasting effects of the modifications and improvements?[13]

Levels of Evaluation

Levels of evaluation are presented here and shown in Figure 10.3. They range from simple to complex and from specific to general in terms of ease of accomplishment. They are presented in levels to show a potential progression in the evaluation process, however, they do not function or exist independently of each other. There is overlap and interdependence between the levels. Overall evaluation of the program is important. Phases or segments of the program also are

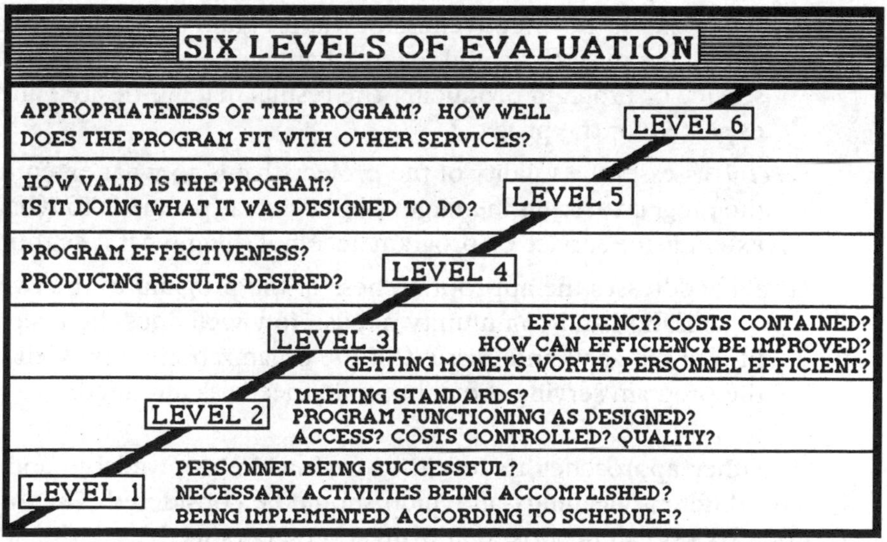

FIGURE 10.3. *Levels of Evaluation*

important to evaluate. Levels of evaluation can be used in the various phases of services or programs.[10,11]

Level 1 focuses on the personnel—what they do on the job, and how they contribute to efficient work flow and overall conduct on the job. This level focuses on important activities necessary to accomplish the program goals and objectives. At this level, the planner and manager wants to know if the program or service is going as it should. Level 1 is where the assessment of the implementation process is conducted. Is the project or service being implemented according to the timeline and the planned schedule? Are the activities of the project going the way they were planned?

Level 2 is used to determine if the project or service is functioning as it was planned, designed, and implemented. Accessibility of the program, cost controls, and overall delivery of the service are reviewed and evaluated.

Level 3 evaluates the efficiency of the service or program and cost-effectiveness of each level or phase is ascertained. Availability and quantity of services is assessed. How can the efficiency of the program be improved in terms of both personnel and cost?

Level 4 looks at the effectiveness of the program or service. This is one of the most basic and essential areas of evaluation. Is the service or program producing the results that are desired and expected for the project?

Level 5 assesses the validity of the project; that is, to what extent is the program serving the target population as planned? To what extent is the service or program accomplishing what it set out to?

Level 6 addresses the appropriateness of the program to the overall organization and community needs. How well does the program fit into the goals and mission of the organization? How well is the program serving the community needs as intended?

Other approaches to levels of evaluation are available and can have different meanings, all which should be considered. The evaluation process can be looked at from several perspectives within a program. These levels relate to and overlap with the six presented above, but they still need to be considered in the context of overall evaluation of a program or service. They are:

1. *Participant, client, patient.* How satisfied is the participant with the service? What are the effects of the service on the client or patient? Are they getting out of the program what they came to receive?
2. *Organization or agency.* What effects has the service or program had on the organization, institution, facility? How well is the staff functioning and how well are the participants being received and treated by the staff? Timelines are considered as well as budgets, personnel, work flow, and related administrative matters.
3. *Process and results.* Are the activities of the program and service or the process of conducting the service producing the results that were expected? Has the program had an impact on the participants and is it serving their needs? Long-term results need to be ascertained as well; over time, what are the consequences of the impact of the service or program on the participants?[10,14]

An evaluation can be designed to assess these issues to see if the organization is being effective in providing the service. It also can determine if the community or organization is getting what it expected. In addition, the effect of the service or program on the participant can be assessed.[9,13] Table 10.2 lists items to use to do an evaluation.[14,15]

Management Issues in Evaluation

For management, the evaluation process may become clouded and may lack direction if not clearly established at the beginning of the planning process. For a successful evaluation process, one member of the planning or management team should be assigned the evaluation responsibility as a part of their regular administrative duties. A task force or committee could be set up to guide the evaluation process; however, one individual should have the responsibility for the process to ensure that it is conducted and completed. Table 10.3 lists some evaluation process "dos and don'ts."[15]

TABLE 10.2. *Items to Use for the Evaluation Process*

Testing (written or oral)	Knowledge
	Attitude
	Behavior
Interviews	Surveys
	In-depth interviews
	Opinion polls
	Group interviews
	Focus groups
	Comparison groups
	Profile development
	Expert opinion
Reports	Medical records and charts
	Special studies
Observations	Professional on-site by trained evaluators
	Checklists
	Guides
	"Yes/no" or "did/did not" evaluations
Samples	Observe examples
	Assess the product or outcomes
Screening results	Compare clinical and paper-and-pencil tests
	Compare pretests to posttests
Questionnaires	Use pretest and posttest comparisons
Goals and Objectives	Use to determine whether goals and objectives and the expected outcomes from them are reached

Feedback

A commonly used model that is useful in understanding the evaluation and feedback process is the *systems model.* (See Figure 10.4.) The systems approach relies on these four processes:

1. Inputs
2. Process
3. Outputs
4. Feedback

TABLE 10.3. *"Dos" and "Don'ts" for Management of the Evaluation Process*

Dos

- Involve the person responsible for evaluation early in the planning process.
- Plan for evaluation early in the planning process.
- Conduct a systematic evaluation and use a planned evaluation process.
- Involve people affected by the evaluation to participate in the planning and carrying it out.
- Coordinate the evaluation effort with all phases of the program and all levels of personnel.

Don'ts

- Don't use sophisticated and complex evaluation approaches and techniques if others work just as well; seek the simple approach first.
- Don't attempt an evaluation or set up the evaluation process if resources to conduct it are lacking.
- Don't use overkill in the evaluation process; use the level, amount, type, and approach that is appropriate for the situation.
- Don't be reluctant to ask elementary, simple, and straightforward questions.
- Don't be overconfident in objective evaluations; do not ignore subjective inputs such as participants, comments and observations.

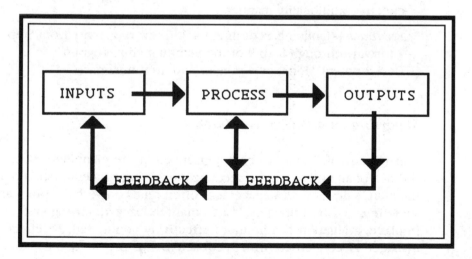

FIGURE 10.4. *Systems Model Showing Feedback Loop Used in the Evaluation Process*

The systems model shows the direction of progress in activities of most projects, planning, or program development. The model in itself can be applied in a general sense to the overall planning process and management. It also can be applied to various or individual phases within the program development process, from need assessments to the implementation process and evaluation.

Using the overall Planning and Program Development Model as presented in this book and applying it to the systems model, in a general manner including feedback, is presented below. (Compare this to Figure 10.3 and the model at the beginning of the book.)

Inputs—Internal assessment, external assessment, goals and objectives for the need assessments, findings of the need assessment, goals and objectives for program development and planning/implementation, and so on.

Process—Conducting the internal assessments, writing the goals and objectives, conducting the planning process, setting priorities, step-by-step activities, developing timelines, implementing the project, and so on.

Outputs—Successful implementation, ongoing success of the project, successful management of the service or program, clients or patients receiving the service in an efficient, effective, and quality manner.

Feedback—Ongoing: returning back to every activity from Step 2 forward through Step 9 of the Planning and Program Development Model on a regular and continual basis.

Reporting as a Part of Feedback

A major downfall that can be experienced in the planning process is the lack of an evaluation and feedback reporting process/system once the plan is developed. Management often relies on verbal reports and sometimes written updates. If a formal feedback reporting system is in place, evaluation can be more effectively conducted. An effective manager is concerned with feedback being provided on a timely basis.[4]

PLANNING QUESTIONS

☐ Are the feedback reports coming often enough to allow for response and if needed, change by management?

☐ Are the feedback reports coming in soon enough after something occurs to allow for an analysis and a planned effective solution?

☐ Is the feedback comprehensive, and does it cover all key elements of the plan and the program?

☐ Is the feedback clear and to the point enough to allow management to respond appropriately?

☐ Is the feedback report provided in a format so that the problem reflects its effect on other aspects or elements of the project?

☐ Does the report emphasize the problem spots, enabling the manager to quickly see the problem and intervene in a timely and effective manner?[4]

☐ Generally, is feedback frequent enough and quick enough to enable the manager to effectively deal with problems that arise?

References

1. Bloch, A. *Murphy's Law, Book Three.* Los Angeles: Price/Stern/Sloan, 1982.
2. Bloch, A. *Murphy's Law, Book Two.* Los Angeles: Price/Stern/Sloan, 1981.
3. Timmreck, T. C. *Dictionary of Health Services Management.* Owings Mills, MD: National Health Publishing, 1987.
4. O'Donnell, M. P. and Ainsworth, T. *Health Promotion in the Workplace.* New York: Wiley, 1984.
5. Green, L. W. and Kreuter M. W. *Health Promotion Planning: An Educational and Environmental Approach.* Mountain View, CA: Mayfield Publishing, 1991.
6. Parkinson, R. *Managing Health Promotion in the Workplace.* Mountain View, CA: Mayfield Publishing, 1982.
7. Green, L. W. and Lewis, F. M. *Measurement and Evaluation in Health Education and Health Promotion.* Mountain View, CA: Mayfield Publishing, 1986.

8. Cole, G. E., et al. "Addressing Problems in Evaluating Health-Relevant Programs Through Systematic Planning and Evaluation," *Risk: Health Safety and Environment*, Vol. 37, No. 6, Winter 1995.

9. Dignan, M. B. and Carr, P. A. *Introduction to Program Planning: A Basic Text for Community Health Education.* Philadelphia: Lea & Febiger, 1981.

10. Blum, H. L. *Planning for Health: Development and Application of Social Change Theory.* New York: Human Sciences Press, 1974.

11. Bergwall, D. F., Reeves, P. N., and Woodside, N. B. *Introduction to Health Planning.* Washington, DC: Information Resources Press, 1974.

12. Spiegel, A. D. and Hyman, H. H. *Basic Health Planning Methods.* Germantown, MD: Aspen Publishing, 1978.

13. Shortell, S. M. and Richardson, W. C. *Health Program Evaluation.* St. Louis: Mosby, 1978.

14. Nutt, P. C. *Planning Methods for Health and Related Organizations.* New York: Wiley, 1984.

Appendix A

Sample Budget for Use in Program Development and Planning

Total for the project	Total $100,671.00	Total requested $78,362.00	Total donated $22,308.00
I. Personnel (Total)	$77,762.00	$58,479.00	$19,283.00
A. Salaries and wages	$49,950.00	$43,200.00	$6,750.00
B. Fringe benefits	$12,248.00	$10,479.00	$1,669.00
C. Consultants and contracts	$15,664.00	$4,800.00	$10,846.00
II. Nonpersonnel (Total)	$22,908.00	$19,883.00	$3,025.00
A. Space—Office, storage, clinic, reception	$12,300.00	$9,900.00	$2,400.00
B. Equipment lease, rent, purchase, maintenance	$2,710.00	$2,085.00	$625.00
C. Supplies, materials, copying	$1,287.00	$1,287.00	-0-
D. Travel and per diem	$1,761.00	$1,761.00	-0-
E. Telephone, computer lines, and utilities	$3,500.00	$3,500.00	-0-
F. Miscellaneous expenses	$1,350.00	$1,350.00	-0-

NOTE: Donated costs are commonly included when making budgets for grants, or in-house requests. Donated costs may be excluded from regular budgets that are not grant oriented.

SOURCE: Adapted from Kiritz, N. J. "Program Planning and Proposal Writing." Published by The Grantsman Center, Los Angeles, 1980.

Items to Remember and Consider When Making Out a Budget

Personnel

Are the personnel full-time or part-time? If part-time, then only the percentage that is being contributed to the project should be listed and any time provided by the organization is listed as "donated time."

Employee-related costs or fringe benefits need to be considered and calculated. Most often these account for about 28 to 35 percent of the personnel costs and the personnel budget. Fringe benefits must be included in the budget and considered as a part of the salary. Fringe benefits include: SUI, workers' compensation, FICA, health and dental insurance, vacation, sick leave or paid time off (PTO), disability insurance, retirement, and so on.

Nonpersonnel

Office space and other space calculated at per square foot per year. Rent, lease or purchase of equipment? What is the best financially for the budget over time?

Travel and per diem should not be overlooked for all persons who need to travel. Mileage should be calculated at the going IRS rates. Telephone and utilities: Don't overlook fax expenses, mobile phones, or computer phone line hook-ups, as well as the usual utilities and telephone expenses. (Phone purchases are listed under equipment.)

Miscellaneous expenses can include memberships in professional organizations, accreditation costs, postage, copying, license fees, and the like.

Appendix B

Suggested Format and Outline for Health Plan/Planning Report

Section I

Mission statement
Introduction
(This area covers general issues and the general need for the project.)

Section II

Goals
Objectives

Section III

Background and justification (detailed overview of the issues and concerns)
Literature review (of problems and concerns)

Section IV

Need and justification (results of need assessments and findings, and so on)
Demographics (profile of target population)
Assessment of existing resources
Charts, graphs, maps, and the like

Section V

Facilities needed
Services offered
Contracts needed

Section VI

Program development and implementation goals and objectives
Implementation plan (the plan of action)
Timelines
Activities (for example, responsibilities set forth)

Section VII

Evaluation and feedback process

Section VIII

Recommendations (to administration or board of directors)

Bibliography/References

Appendix C

Criteria for the Development of Health Promotion and Health Education Programs

Criterion No. 1: A health promotion program should address one or more risk factors that are carefully defined, measurable, modifiable, and prevalent among the target group. Factors that constitute a threat to the health status and the quality of life of the target group members should be selected. Issues to resolve include:

- How specifically can each risk factor be defined?
- How prevalent is the selected risk factor within the chosen target group(s)?
- How may the incidence and prevalence of the selected risk factor be measured?
- Is the risk factor amenable to change? Is the risk factor modifiable, or can its prevalence or incidence be reduced?
- Would reduction of the risk factor improve the health status and/or quality of life of the members of the target group?
- Do the risk factors chosen as program emphases reflect the priorities and preferences of the target group and the community as a whole?

Criterion No. 2: A health promotion program should consider and reflect the special characteristics, needs, and preferences of the target group(s). Issues to resolve include:

- Can the size and composition of the population at high risk be described and defined?
- Does the selected intervention reflect the priorities and preferences of the target group(s) and the community as a whole?
- Are there primary and secondary target groups for the intervention program?
- Are there special problems of access among the members of a particular group with respect to the proposed health promotion program?
- Will special efforts be required to attract and sustain the participation of members of the target group in the intervention program? If so, what efforts?
- Has the target group been sufficiently involved in planning the proposed intervention? What degree of involvement is needed?

- Are there special political problems associated with the selection of a particular target group and for the intervention selected to be used by an organization? Are outside groups going to have concerns and need to have input into the use of the chosen intervention? Are there strong positive or negative public attitudes toward the intervention (such as with sex education or birth control programs)?

Criterion No. 3: Health promotion programs should include interventions that clearly and effectively reduce a targeted risk factor and are appropriate for a particular setting. Issues to resolve include:

- What types of interventions are known to be most effective in dealing with the risk factors selected for program emphasis among populations similar to the chosen target groups?

- What evidence supports or proves the effectiveness of the chosen intervention? Are there any related, carefully designed experimental studies or other types of potential program evaluations?

- Does available evidence document the effectiveness of the selected intervention in similar settings and among similar target groups?

- What is the nature of approach of the proposed intervention? What are the critical elements of the intervention? Must any part of the intervention be implemented under special circumstances or through certain sequential steps?

- What happens if only part of the intervention is carried out?

- Are licensed personnel required to carry out the intervention (such as doctors to prescribe nicotine patches or gum)?

- Based on previous experience, what is the degree of anticipated difficulty or ease of applying the proposed intervention?

Criterion No. 4: Health promotion programs should identify and implement interventions that make optimum use of available resources. Issues to resolve include:

- What levels of organizational resources, including personnel, are required to plan, initiate, implement, manage, maintain, and sustain the health promotion program in the proposed setting?

- What are the estimated costs (monetary and nonmonetary), benefits, and other effects of the proposed intervention?
- Are there special funding requirements for planning, implementing, managing, and maintaining the program in the proposed setting?
- Are there existing community resources that might be used as part of the program initiative, thereby reducing initial resource requirements for the proposed program? What impact would use of these resources have on program effectiveness?

Criterion No. 5: From the outset, a health promotion program should be organized, planned and implemented in such a way that its operation and effects can be evaluated. Issues to resolve include:

- Are there baseline measures of the prevalence (current extent) and incidence (rate of occurrence) of the identified risk factors among members of the target group?
- Are careful records kept in an objective manner throughout the program by which to establish baselines of data and measure the extent of participation in the program by target group members when the intervention or program is completed?
- Is it possible, feasible, or ethical to randomly assign target exposure to the intervention program? If not, can a control group be found, which has characteristics common to the participant group but that is not exposed to the program, to use for research comparison? Can the control group provide enough information relative to the risk factors selected for intervention within the target group?
- Are there individuals or organizations with competency in program evaluation available to assist with the necessary tasks?
- Is careful consideration given to evaluation expectations and requirements at the beginning of the program? Can program objectives be defined in measurable terms before the program starts?

Appendix D

Internet Health Planning and Program Development Resources

Administration on Aging = www.aoa.dhhs.gov

Administration for Children and Families (ACF) = www.acf.dhhs.gov

Agency for Health Care Policy and Research = www.ahcpr.gov

Agency for Healthcare Research and Quality = www.ahrq.gov

Alcohol and Drug Information, National Clearinghouse =
   www.health.org

American Association of Retired Persons (AARP) = www.aarp.com

American Cancer Society = www.cancer.org

American Diabetes Association = www.diabetes.org
   California Affiliate = www.diabetes.org/adaca

American Health Quality Association = www.ahqa.org

American Heart Association = www.americanheart.org

Bureau of Justices Statistics = www.ojp.usdoj.gov/bjs

Bureau of Labor Statistics = www.bls.gov

California Demographic Research Unit of the Department of Finance =
   www.dof.ca.gov

California Department of Health and Human Services =
   www.chhs.ca.gov

California Department of Health Services = www.dhs.cahwnet.gov

Census Bureau = www.census.gov

Census Lookup = www.census.gov/cdrom/lookup

Centers for Disease Control and Prevention = www.cdc.gov

Common Wealth Fund = www.cmwf.org

Community Tool Box (Program Evaluation) =
   ctb.lsi.ukans.edu/tools/EN/section_1338.htm

Demography and Population Studies =
   demography.anu.edu.au/virtualLibrary

Demography, US = www.ciesin.org/datasets/us-demog/
   us-demog-home.html

Department of Health and Human Services (Federal) =
   www.os.dhhs.gov

Drug and Alcohol Information, National Clearinghouse =
   www.health.org

Environmental Sciences Division (ESD) of Oak Ridge National
   Laboratory (ORNL) = www.esd.ornl.gov

Epidemiology Program Office (for CDC) = www.cdc.gov/epo

Federal Register = www.access.gpo.gov/sudocs/aces/aces140.html

Health Care Financing Administration (Medicare and Medicaid) =
   www.hcfa.gov

Health Resources and Services Administration = www.hrsa.gov
Healthy City, Building = www.imaginewhatif.com/Pages/
  toolkit.html
Healthy People 2010 = www.health.gov/healthypeople
Kaiser Family Foundation = www.kff.org
Library of Congress Services and Publications = lcweb.loc.gov
Links to federal government sites =
  www.usdoj.gov/02organizations/02 6.html
Morbidity and Mortality Weekly Report = www.cdc.gov/mmwr
National Center for Chronic Disease Prevention and Health
  Promotion = www.cdc.gov/nccdphp
National Center for Complementary and Alternative Medicine =
  nccam.nih.gov
National Center for Health Statistics = www.cdc.gov/nchs
National Center for Health Promotion = www.welltech.com/nchp
National Center for Infectious Diseases = www.cdc.gov/ncidod
National Center for Injury Prevention and Control =
  www.cdc.gov/ncipc/ncipchm.htm
National Center for Research Resources = www.ncrr.nih.gov
National Council on Aging = www.ncoa.org
National Health Information Center = nhic-nt.health.org
National Institute on Aging = www.nih.gov/nia
National Institute on Alcohol Abuse and Alcoholism (NIAAA) =
  www.niaaa.nih.gov
National Institute of Child Health and Human Development =
  www.nichd.nih.gov
National Institute on Drug Abuse = www.nida.nih.gov
National Institute of Health = www.nih.gov
National Institute of General Medical Sciences =
  www.nigms.nih.gov
National Library of Medicine = www.nlm.nih.gov
National Institute of Mental Health = www.nimh.nih.gov
National Institute for Occupation Safety and Health =
  www.cdc.gov/niosh
Office of Disease Prevention and Health Promotion =
  odphp.osophs.dhhs.gov
Office of Global Health (CDC) = www.cdc.gov/ogh
Office of Minority Health = www.omhrc.gov
Office of Population Research = Opr.princeton.edu

Office of Women's Health (CDC) = www.cdc.gov.health/
womensmenu.htm

Partnerships Against Violence Network = www.pavnet.org

Population Reference Bureau = www.prb.org

Public Health Practice Program Office = www.phppo.cdc.gov.

Rand Health Science Program = www.rand.org/organization/health

Robert Wood Johnson Foundation = www.rwjf.org

Statistical briefs—Census Bureau = www.census.gov/ftp/pub/
apsd/www/statbrief

State and local governments on the Net = www.piperinfo.com/state/
index.cfm

Substance Abuse and Mental Health Services Administration =
www.samhsa.gov

U.S. Government Printing Office = www.access.gpo.gov/index.html

U.S. Public Health Service = phs.os.dhhs.gov/phs/phs.html

World Health Organization = www.who.int

Appendix E

Epi Info

What Is Epi Info 2000?

Epi Info is a series of programs for Microsoft Windows 95, 98, NT, and 2000 for use by public health professionals in conducting outbreak investigations, managing databases for public health surveillance and other tasks, and general database and statistics applications. With Epi Info and a personal computer, physicians, epidemiologists, and other public health and medical workers can rapidly develop a questionnaire or form, customize the data entry process, and enter and analyze data.

Tables are produced with simple commands such as READ, FREQ, LIST, TABLES, and GRAPH. A component called Epi Map displays geographic maps with data from Epi Info. Epi Info is in the public domain and can be downloaded from the Internet. CD-ROM copies and printed manuals are expected to be available from private vendors.

The first version of Epi Info was released in 1985. A study in 1997 documented 145,000 copies of the DOS versions of Epi Info and Epi Map in 117 countries. The DOS manual and/or programs have been translated into 13 non-English languages. Epi Info 2000 is an entirely new series of programs for Microsoft Windows 95, 98, NT, and 2000, written in Visual Basic, Version 6. It uses the Microsoft Access file format as a gateway to industry database standards. Although Epi Info 2000 data is stored in Microsoft Access files for maximum compatibility with other systems, many other file types can be analyzed, imported, or exported. Epi Info 2000 includes a Geographic Information System (GIS), called Epi Map 2000, built around the MapObjects program from Environmental Sciences Research, Inc., the producers of ArcView. Epi Map is compatible with GIS data from numerous Internet sites in the popular ESRI formats. Epi Info 2000 retains many features of the familiar Epi Info for DOS, while offering Windows strengths such as point-and-click ease of use, graphics, fonts, and painless printing. The programs, documentation, and teaching materials are in the public domain (although "Epi Info" is a CDC trademark) and may be freely copied, distributed, or translated.

Key Features of Epi Info 2000

- Maximum compatibility with industry standards, including:

    4 Microsoft ACCESS and other SQL and ODBC databases

4 Visual Basic, Version 6

4 World Wide Web browsers and HTML

- Extensibility, so that organizations outside CDC can produce additional modules.

Epi Map, an ArcView-compatible GIS

- Logistic regression and Kaplan–Meier survival analysis
- Teaching exercises
- Entirely new, not just a "port" of Epi Info for DOS
- Microsoft Windows 95, 98, NT, and 2000 compatible
- Allows analysis and importation of other file types

System Requirements

- Windows 95, 98, NT, or 2000, with 32 megabytes of RAM—More for NT.
- At least 50 megabytes of free hard disk space.
- A 200-megahertz processor is recommended but not required.

Epi Info Web site address: www.cdc.gov/epiinfo

Appendix F

Epi Map: Geographic Information System (GIS)

An entirely new version of Epi Map is included with Epi Info 2000. The core of the program is the same mapping engine that is used in ArcView, a popular Geographic Information System from Environmental Sciences Research Institute (ESRI), Inc. Although Epi Map does not have all the features of the high-end commercial programs, ArcView and ARC/INFO, it is capable of reading many of the same file formats, allowing users to tap the enormous mapping resources that are offered on the Internet as SHAPE (SHP) files. A catalog of resources is included with Epi Info 2000 to illustrate how these can be found. Epi Map 2000 can display SHAPE files in multiple layers. Each layer can be linked to an Epi Info 2000 data table containing geographic names or codes for the entities of the map. Data for each entity (a count or rate, for example) can be displayed in color/pattern (choropleth) maps as in Epi Map for DOS, or as dots randomly distributed within the map's polygons. New features in Epi Map 2000 allow displaying streets and placing symbols by coordinates. Thus, one can produce a map similar to John Snow's original map of cholera cases and water-pump locations in London.

SOURCE: Adapted from the criteria prepared by an Ad Hoc Work Group of the American Public Health Association.

Index